THE UNFILTERED ENNEAGRAM

THE UNFILTERED
ENNEAGRAM

*A Witty and Wise
Guide to Self-Compassion*

ELIZABETH ORR

CONVERGENT

New York

A Convergent Books Trade Paperback Original

Published in the United States by Convergent Books, an imprint
of Random House, a division of Penguin Random House LLC,
New York.

CONVERGENT BOOKS is a registered trademark and the
Convergent colophon is a trademark of Penguin Random House
LLC.

Grateful acknowledgment is made to HarperCollins Publishers for
permission to adapt text from *The Essential Enneagram* by David
Daniels, M.D., and Virginia A. Price, Ph.D., copyright © 2000
by David N. Daniels, M.D., and Virginia A. Price, Ph.D.
Used by permission of HarperCollins Publishers.

LIBRARY OF CONGRESS CATALOGING-IN-PUBLICATION DATA

Names: Orr, Elizabeth, author.
Title: The unfiltered Enneagram / Elizabeth Orr.
Description: New York, NY: Convergent Books, 2024
Identifiers: LCCN 2023048696 (print) | LCCN 2023048697 (ebook) |
ISBN 9780593593899 (trade paperback) | ISBN 9780593593905 (ebook)
Subjects: LCSH: Enneagram. | Personality assessment. | Self-perception.
Classification: LCC BF698.35.E54 O77 2024 (print) |
LCC BF698.35.E54 (ebook) | DDC 155.2/6—dc23/eng/20231106
LC record available at https://lccn.loc.gov/2023048696
LC ebook record available at https://lccn.loc.gov/2023048697

Printed in the United States of America on acid-free paper

convergentbooks.com

2 4 6 8 9 7 5 3 1

Book design by Fritz Metsch

To my faithful and funny-as-hell Type Six friend
K. Virginia Christman:

I hope this book can stand as evidence to you that sometimes the things you suspect will work out well actually do.

And to my brilliant and visionary Type Seven friend
K. Monet Rice:

I hope this book can stand as evidence to you that unapologetically staying in your lane can manifest a reality that's even better than what you imagined was possible.

CONTENTS

PART IV: THE HEAD CENTER

AUTHOR'S NOTE

This Is Not Another Enneagram Book

I'm willing to bet that you picked up this book because you're interested in the Enneagram, so let me come clean to you right off the bat: This is not an Enneagram book. Sure, we're going to talk a lot about the Enneagram, but this book is not principally about the Enneagram.

I didn't write this book because I think there aren't enough resources about the Enneagram out there already. There are, and many of them are excellent. I wrote this book because there will never be enough said, written, or cosmically transmitted about the lifelong work of learning how to love ourselves well. That isn't to say there haven't also been some brilliant things said about the subject of self-compassion—there have! It's just that our world is so full of messages about why we aren't deserving of love that we can't fight against those narratives enough.

Now, the irony isn't lost on me that this book and indeed my reputation, if you're at all familiar with it, aren't warm and cuddly and sweet. In fact, they're quite the opposite. I've built a whole persona and an entire secondary career for myself on being rude to strangers on the internet about their Enneagram Type. So, the idea that I have anything meaningful to contribute to the conversation around self-compassion is one that you'd probably be right to be skeptical of (especially Sixes—although, in all fairness, you were going to be skeptical of me regardless). But let me make my case for how this book, arguably the literary equivalent of a Comedy Central Roast on Enneagram Type, might actually support you in your journey to loving yourself more fully.

WHY SELF-COMPASSION?

In the method for Enneagram typing interviews that I have been trained with, the first three questions ask interviewees to pick adjectives to describe themselves, and the second question asks them to think about the adjectives that someone who absolutely adores them would pick to describe them. When I invite people to see themselves through the loving lens of someone they are close to, the edges of guardedness and formality tend to soften, and the person I am interviewing almost transports from my office or Zoom screen into the warm glow of their loved one's affection for them. It's a really special moment in the interview, and if we didn't have thirty other questions to get through, I would let them linger in it for as long as they'd like.

You know what? We don't even need a typing interview to get the picture I'm trying to illustrate—we can do this right here and right now. Think for a moment about two or three adjectives that you would use to describe yourself, and then imagine the two or three adjectives that someone who holds you in the highest regard might use to describe you.

Those fleeting experiences of knowing that we are deeply known and loved by someone else can feel like a far cry from our present reality. I'm not breaking radical ground here in saying that an enormous part of the misery that makes up what my therapist calls "the human condition" is a relentless onslaught of mixed messages about whether we are deserving of love. Multiple multibillion-dollar industries are built on the backs of our insecurities, with makeup, fast-fashion clothing trends, extreme diet and fitness plans, wellness programs, and plastic surgery all inundating us with the message that exactly how we are right now is unacceptable and must be remedied immediately. Because these industries are so profitable, we don't have to look very hard to find another reason why we aren't worthy of love.

In a cold and predatory world that exploits our fears about ourselves (could I sound any more like an Eight right now, jeez), the intentional act of being compassionate and noticing that which is deserving of love in others is a hopeful lifeline to us all. And this may sound counterintuitive to everything I've just said, but stick with me here: The best place to start cultivating more compassion is with yourself. Yes it's also probably one of the most difficult places to start—since we've learned to internalize all those nasty messages about how awful we are and how ashamed we should be for being less than perfect—but that's exactly why starting with ourselves is so vital. When you can counter the internal voice that calls you stupid for an honest mistake with a gentle reminder that you're doing the best you can and that's not stupid at all, then not only are you taking back your own agency from these "beauty and wellness" business bullies, but you are also helping to teach yourself how to spot that which is deserving of love, despite the cruel landscape of self-inflicted criticisms. And when you can hone that skill with yourself, the person you never get a break from, it becomes easier and easier to offer that practice of generosity to others as well.

Self-compassion is not self-indulgence; it is the most badass practice we have available to us for survival in what often feels like a cold and uncaring world. Becoming our own hype-people isn't self-serving; if anything, self-compassion is one of the greatest ways we can cultivate more compassion in the world, helping us learn to focus on that which is deserving of love within ourselves, which clarifies our perspective and helps us see those things more easily in others. And far from our exhausting attempts to fit ourselves into a standard that is being sold to us by the vultures of societally acceptable norms, self-compassion is grounded in honesty and humility. Just like the love of someone we trust, self-compassion says, "Sure, I'm not perfect, but I'm certainly good enough to deserve experiencing love."

I'm not saying self-compassion is an easy practice, but it is just that, a *practice,* a set of muscles that can be strengthened with consistency over time. When we dedicate ourselves to practicing compassion for ourselves, that warm and safe feeling of knowing that we are deserving of love is available to us and to the people around us at all times. Self-compassion is the source of the compassion we give to others, and it is the lens through which we can begin to imagine and build a kinder, more compassionate world. *That*, friends, is what I wrote this book about.

WHY THE ENNEAGRAM?

Okay, so, self-compassion—essential. Got it. Why the Enneagram, then? Before I was ever an author, an Enneagram nerd, or even an associate university chaplain (my day job—go Deacs!), I was a meat-headed jock. So, if you'll humor me, I'm going to offer you an answer in the form of a sports analogy: If the goal of this book is to strengthen our muscles of self-love and self-compassion, think of the Enneagram as barbells and cardio machines in a gym. The Enneagram is the equipment with which we're going to strengthen those muscles. And just like on leg day, plan on being sore for a few days afterward.

If you're at all familiar with the Enneagram (and if you're not, don't worry—you will be by the end of this book), then you already know that it's an amazing tool to develop our muscles of self-awareness and compassion for ourselves and others. But that isn't what first draws us into the Enneagram. It's the borderline creepy experience of having something describe our innermost thoughts and fears with an uncanny precision. That unsettling experience of recognizing ourselves in a Type description is both exhilarating and eerie and is often the conversion experience that pitches us headfirst into the baptismal font of full-blown born-again Enneagram evangelism.

Sadly, that initial rush of feeling recognized is such a delicious high that most people end up stuck in the cycle of chasing that feeling by consuming all the memes and podcasts they can just to get another glimpse of themselves in the mystical Enneagram mirror. That's not entirely their fault, though. Quality Enneagram trainings are both expensive and time consuming, and without a foundational understanding of the traditional Enneagram, many of the classic books about the Enneagram can feel too intellectual and dense to absorb in a meaningful and actionable way. With trainings and books as inaccessible and hard to digest as they are, many people are left out in the wilderness, patching together piecemeal understandings of the Enneagram, carrying around an anemic, generic version of one of the most powerful and practical personal development tools out there.

My observation is that the larger cultural conversation about the Enneagram is, unfortunately, relatively flat and one-dimensional. There is a hyper-fixation on the Types and reductive, if juicy, descriptions that don't lend themselves to anything substantive as it relates to transformation and liberation from our own bad behavior. Admittedly, it's thrilling to see ourselves described in a paragraph or a meme, but if those descriptions don't disrupt our lives a little bit, then who cares?

Compounding all of this, there is an inner circle of Enneagram gatekeepers who often turn up their noses at attempts to present the Enneagram in more modern, approachable terms for broader access. To build on our gym metaphor, this inner circle acts a lot like the folks who complain about the crowd of new gym-goers in early January. They make the Enneagram world inhospitable, and they take the Enneagram and, even worse, themselves so seriously that it remains not only unapproachable but also unappealing.

So that's the state of the Enneagram world: Either it's too light and fluffy, lacking substance, depth, and teeth, or it's too inaccessible and serious, condescending to anyone who hasn't already spent thousands of dollars and thousands of years in trainings.

The world tells us we aren't deserving of love, and we have an amazing tool to support our radical revolt against that garbage message—but tragically, most people don't understand or know how to use it.

ALL RIGHT, BUT WHY ARE YOU BEING SO RUDE?

It was this weird whiplash between cotton-candy-sweet and serious-as-a-heart-attack that inspired me to create @RudeAssEnneagram in the first place. In addition to the two extremes I just mentioned, there is a layer of religion that overlays much of the substantive Enneagram content. And while that is neither good nor bad, as a chaplain in the field of higher education, I actually have the professional chops to tell you with some authority that many millennials and Gen Zers are turned off by traditional models of religion. If someone is already reluctant to approach something religious, they might pass up the Enneagram *because* of its religious associations.

So, in an effort to create a new port of entry for the Enneagram, I decided to make use of my snarky, smart-ass sense of humor, and @RudeAssEnneagram was born. For a lot of people, my Instagram account became a place where they could not only recognize themselves in my posts but also laugh at themselves at the same time. This brings me to another foundational belief that I hold, one that was an enormous motivation for me in starting @RudeAssEnneagram and eventually in writing this book: Humor isn't just an important part of our self-compassion journey; it's actually absolutely *essential.*

At some point on its journey from this semi-secretive framework that was talked about in living rooms (how I was introduced to it) to its current status as the darling of corporate professional development topics, we kind of lost the plot of the Enneagram. At its inception in the early 1920s, it was a very basic system for identifying our internal barriers to balance and enlightenment. As a matter of fact, the earliest iteration of the Enneagram described three distinctive "idiots," each with their own characteristic brand of bunk. At its core, the Enneagram was never about identifying with ego-stroking titles and personality traits like the Giver, the Loyal Skeptic, or the Peacemaker; the Enneagram was principally about revealing our shadow side, the ways in which we unconsciously put ourselves and our loved ones through a whole lot of hell in the name of self-protection.

So, if the Enneagram isn't some cute personality summary but instead is a brutal indictment of how we engineer and participate in a lot of our own misery, then the need for a sense of humor about ourselves should become obvious. The road to self-compassion is lined with some pretty difficult truths about ourselves. But I believe this with every fiber of my being: Humor can be the bridge that gets us from hanging our heads in shame at the harm we're capable of causing to holding these patterns of crap with compassion and understanding, while releasing ourselves from their grip.

Part I

INTRODUCTION

ENNEAGRAM HISTORY
AND OVERVIEW OF THE TYPES

Look, let's level with each other, all right? I know it's more likely than not that you aren't reading this chapter in the order that I intended it to be read; you're coming back to it after having skipped ahead to the chapter about your Type or the Type of the person who finally convinced you (or wore you down enough) to read a book about the Enneagram. I'd love to think that my writing about the Enneagram is like me and needs no introduction, but I can't go asking the Twos to practice humility if I'm not willing to give those muscles a lil stretch myself once in a while. So, each Type's chapter *is* going to make a lot more sense and land in a more practical way when you have the bird's-eye view as a point of reference. Now that you've made your way back here, the real fun can begin.

It's hard to swing a cat around these days without hitting the Enneagram. From corporate team-building workshops to dating app profiles, it feels like it's everywhere, and there's a good chance that someone in your life is a full-fledged member of the Enneagram cult. If you've somehow managed to escape the grip of the Enneagram-enthused to this point, well . . . welcome to the top of the rabbit hole.

A VERY BRIEF HISTORY OF THE ENNEAGRAM

One of the first things that most of us hear about the Enneagram is a big ole myth. I doubt there was any intentional deception happening with the propagation of the notion that the Enneagram is ancient, but sometime during the telephone game of oral tradition, the Enneagram being as old as the mountains became canon in the narrative, and it's been next to impossible to update the script. I'm here to tell you today, though, dear reader, that the Enneagram is only as vintage as Pyrex bakeware: old enough to be at home (and a killer find if you stumble across it!) in a charming antique shop. But to claim that the Enneagram is some ancient, primordial secret that has been passed down from generation to generation is . . . a stretch, y'all.

In reality, the first public reference to the Enneagram dates back to the 1920s, when George Gurdjieff, a teacher, philosopher, and spiritually curious cat, referenced the symbol in his work in psychology, spirituality, self-awareness, and a whole host of other areas. At no point did Gurdjieff ever talk about nine distinct personality Types. Instead, he used the Enneagram symbol to illustrate the dynamism of our world, nature, daily life, and art—showing that the world around us has something to teach us about ourselves and that enlightenment is less of a static destination or goal and more of a moving target, available to us in every moment. The most definitive DNA strand in his body of work that turns up in the genetic makeup of the modern-day Enneagram is his contribution to the Centers of Intelligence.

Now, for the sake of brevity, I'm about to do the story of Gurdjieff's travels a real injustice by trimming it down. But for our purposes, you probably don't need the play-by-play nor my color commentary, so here's the SparkNotes version: Hungry for enlightenment, Gurdjieff immersed himself in the spiritual circles of the Yogi, monk, and fakir communities, studying their holy practices of meditation, faithful religious sacrifice, and asceticism, respectively.

By committing himself to these communities and their unique practices, Gurdjieff came away with two distinct insights (at least as far as the Enneagram is concerned). First, that each of these approaches was very singularly focused on either the mind, the heart, or the body, yet he was able to attune himself to each. His experience signaled to him that *every* person has the capacity to do the same: We all possess active mental, emotional, and somatic ways of perceiving the world around us.

This was all well and lovely, except that each of these approaches demanded a full retreat from the world and daily life, which is inaccessible to most folks (this is Gurdjieff's second insight, for those keeping score at home). Not only that, but enlightenment for enlightenment's sake also ends up being an exercise in vanity. If an enlightened ego falls in the forest and there's no one there to hear it and benefit from a more compassionate consciousness, then who cares?

Armed with his lived experiences of these three paths to enlightenment, Gurdjieff set off to blaze his own more accessible trail, a trail that became known as the Fourth Way. This Fourth Way allowed people to engage and remain in their regular lives by focusing their attention on their bodily felt sensations, their affective movements, and their intellectual thoughts. These three Centers of Intelligence form the very foundation of the Enneagram, which would only later be built up into the nine Types that we know and love today. The 1960s and 1970s saw teachers like Oscar Ichazo and Claudio Naranjo integrate the Enneagram into modern psychology. The 1980s and 1990s saw the Enneagram in conversation with spiritual direction, thanks to Robert Ochs and the Jesuit order, as well as the Enneagram gaining a wider audience through formalized training programs and the publication of the first books on the topic. And of course, with the advent of social media, the almost inevitable explosion of popularity that the Enneagram is currently enjoying brings us to the present day.

So, we know the Enneagram *isn't* ancient, like everyone says, but what in the heck is it, then? Most people's understanding of the Enneagram begins and ends with it functioning as another personality typing system. In just about every Enneagram workshop I've ever facilitated, at least one participant is armed with a serious case of suspicion about the validity of the Enneagram. In all fairness to the Enneagram-resistant crowd, the Enneagram deals with our personalities, and justifiably, a lot of people bristle at personality typing systems, because, at first pass, the notion that all of humanity can be reduced to just nine archetypes flies in the face of our universal feeling of terminal uniqueness. The reality is, though, that the Enneagram is *not* just another personality typing system.

I know, I know—I'm still answering this question about what the Enneagram *is* by offering examples of what it *isn't*. It isn't ancient; it isn't just a personality typing system. Cool, Liz, but can we land the plane? **The Enneagram is a framework that reveals the places where we've built up brick-wall barriers to being seen and known. It doesn't tell us who we are so much as it shows us how we get in our own way.**

All right, we've covered enough background—why don't we take a quick spin around the Enneagram so you can see for yourself what I'm rambling on about?

THE GUT CENTER

The Gut Center of the Enneagram, sometimes referred to as the Anger Triad, consists of Types Eight, Nine, and One. Characterized by big somatic energy and an even bigger attitude about their autonomy and their boundaries, these three Types share a natural strength and a supernatural rage.

Type Eight

Often referred to as the Challenger or the Protector, Eights are the self-appointed head honcho of the Enneagram, boasting razor-sharp instincts and a confidence in themselves that can border on arrogance when they're not careful, which they aren't very often. High on intensity and low on tolerance for their own sensitivity and tenderness, Eights empower others at their best and intimidate at their worst, mistaking aggression and belligerence for strength and autonomy. Constantly walking around looking for a fight and instigating one when they come up empty handed, Eights turn conversation into a contact sport, hiding their soft lil hearts under the armor of controversial opinions and contempt for social niceties.

Type Nine

Typically named the Peacemaker or the Mediator, Nines are the human version of a chill pill, bringing the emotional temperature of the room down from conflicted and contentious to calm and comfortable with just their grounded presence. Unassuming and unobtrusive, Nines seem easygoing on the surface, but under their mellow façade, they're arguably the most stubborn Type, exerting their strength by avoidance and disengagement, fleeing the scene of tension and strife—lest they have to face their inner rage at their pattern of self-forgetting that they have numbed themselves to for years.

Type One

Ones are regularly granted the title of the Perfectionist but will just as regularly correct you with their preferred archetypal name for their Type. Highly principled and stubbornly hopeful about the possibility of being and doing better, Ones are at their best when they can lead by their virtuous example, while still finding the space to be silly and playful. Unfortunately, Ones are more often known as the kind of cooks who can't take the heat but still refuse to get out of the kitchen, dishing out criticism to others that they recoil from when it's given back to them. Self-righteous and rigid in the standards they hold, Ones nurse grudges like nobody else, especially when they're the ones they're beefing with. More concerned about being right than getting it right, Ones are adamantly convinced that they know best and at the same time deeply convicted that their humanity is evidence of a deep inner pollution that degrades everything they do, despite their best efforts and honorable intentions.

THE HEART CENTER

The Heart Center of the Enneagram, occasionally called the Shame Triad, is made up of Types Two, Three, and Four. Warm, relational, and impermanent in their sense of self, seeking it out in their relationships and roles, these Types are haunted by the questions "Who am I, and is that person even worthy of love?"

Type Two

Twos are the sweethearts of the Enneagram. Usually known as the Giver or the Nurturer, they're famous for their ability to make others feel well loved. That said, there are some serious strings attached to Twos' generosity. Ping-ponging between a bloated sense of self-importance—inflated by how much they do for others and how little they survive on in return—and deeper doubts that they deserve love, Twos give in order to get, using their natural ability to be tender and sweet to manipulate others into giving them the love they refuse to extend to themselves.

Type Three

The Threes' archetypal name, the Performer, gives away their cardinal sin—putting on one helluva show, an ever-changing production for their ever-changing audience. Charming and competent, Threes spend more time building up their résumés than their sense of self, constructing their identity with the bricks of external markers of success, rather than less obviously admirable things like their own values. Confusing who they are with what they do, Threes only appear shameless in their pattern of self-promotion, the humiliation of surviving on external validation relentlessly pressing them onward in their search for the next hit of praise.

Type Four

Fours have been crowned as the Romantic or the Artist of the Enneagram. Rich in creativity, imagination, and emotional whiplash, they're just as quick to loudly and dramatically declare their affection as they are to rescind it—in equally loud and dramatic fashion. Looking for someone or something outside themselves to complete them, Fours perpetually set themselves up for disappointment, letting their impressive imaginations run wild, turning the object of their desire into a projection screen for everything they believe themselves to be missing. Fours are happiest when they can brood in peace, savoring the emotional experience of melancholy and envy and the meaning it helps them craft.

THE HEAD CENTER

The Head Center of the Enneagram, also known as the Fear Triad, is where Types Five, Six, and Seven reside. With a focus that orients them toward the future and agile, precise, and curious minds that generate something new out of what they take in, the Head Center Types are plagued by trust issues, angsty and fearful that they can't depend on others or themselves for whatever lies ahead.

Type Five

The Fives' relationship to the Head Center is obvious from their archetypal name of the Investigator to the depths of research that they will submerge themselves in. Appearing emotionally even-keeled and rational, they hide tender, sensitive hearts underneath the logic that is desperately trying to avoid becoming overwhelmed by its own affectability, let alone the intrusive and unpredictable emotions of others. Constantly vigilant against unexpected demands, Fives can become stingy and withholding, guarding their inner resources with a closefistedness that rivals corporations' tax-paying tendencies. Despite their lifelong commitment to seeking deeper understanding, Fives refuse to trust in the amount of knowledge and expertise they've accrued, fearing that whatever they haven't yet read will reveal the depths of their ignorance.

Type Six

The Sixes' famous skepticism has earned them the archetypal name of the Devil's Advocate, and their infamous (and unceasing) questioning, doubting, and testing of information that's presented to them have earned them many an exhausted side-eye from friends and colleagues. Sixes are well liked for their disarming sense of humor, their ride-or-die loyalty, and the way they always have Band-Aids, ibuprofen, and other minor emergency provisions when anyone needs them. Mental hyperactivity in the form of anticipating the worst-case scenario and attempting to mitigate it, then rinsing and repeating relentlessly, takes the place of actually facing the thing they're afraid of, ultimately depriving them of the opportunity to see what they're capable of in the face of their fears.

Type Seven

Sevens, the party people of the Enneagram, have earned their archetypal name of the Adventurer with their lifelong pattern of chasing the next thrill. Quick-witted and clever, they're a hoot and a holler to be around, always ready with an outrageous story or side-splitting joke to liven the mood and get the party started. Sevens live fast-paced lives, hopping from one pursuit to the next while the lifeless bodies of the dreams they abandoned at the first hint of boredom or difficulty litter the path behind them, alongside all their excuses as to why those dreams weren't worth actualizing

anyway. Terrified of deprivation but even more terrified of deprivation at the hands of their own limitations, Sevens consume stimulation indiscriminately, attempting to satisfy an appetite that
knows disappointment only after a lifetime of letting the promise
of what could be elevate their expectations to unrealistic heights.

There ya have it. The quick and dirty version of all nine Enneagram
Types. It's these flashy and enticing paragraphs of quick descriptions that are widely available and that often get people hooked on
the Enneagram. Succinct and yet still so all-consuming, these ef-
ficient summaries let us see ourselves in all our awful glory. But in
the pages that follow, we're going to get into the real power of the
Enneagram: *why* we are the way we are.

When we can understand why we are the way we are, we can
extend compassion and perspective to painful memories and patterns, when we were earnestly doing the best that we could in the
moment. When we can see our motivation with clarity and sobriety, we can lay down the protective armor we've taken up in the
service of survival.

I'm not going to promise you that upon finishing this book,
you'll be cured of your worst instincts and defensive knee-jerk reactions, but what I hope is that this book will give you concrete,
objective pieces of the wall that you've built around yourself and
will make it easier to observe those instincts and reactions operating in real time. More than that, I hope that this book will help you
recognize that every time you catch yourself becoming reactive, it's
also an invitation to become present to what is going on within you
so that you can have freedom from the prison of your predictable
patterns and extend compassion to yourself *and* others. Self-
awareness and self-compassion are targets that move every day,
targets that we never get to fully arrive at. But with the knowledge
that the Enneagram grants us, we can get closer.

And that's why the Enneagram is so amazing.

ENNEAGRAM TYPES AS PATTERN-MAKING MACHINERY, NOT PERSONALITY TRAITS

Much of what dominates the most accessible of Enneagram spaces these days are sprawling descriptive paragraphs, and while they are revealing, they tend to be two-dimensional in their presentation of strengths and weaknesses of each Type. Additionally, they are fairly lacking in clarity as to *how* and *why* our Types function the way they do. If we don't understand how and why our ego structure functions, there's not a lot we can do to interrupt it. So, while there will be sprawling descriptive paragraphs in this book, there will also be a very definitive "if this, then that" formula that I hope will help you see the sequence of events that takes place within us. Events that produce and reproduce predictable patterns of emotions, thoughts, and behaviors that ultimately create conflict and frustration in our immediate world and relationships.

One of the best-kept secrets of the Enneagram world—hiding in plain sight within the pages of a little yellow book called *The Essential Enneagram**—is the framework known as the Basic Propositions. Developed by Dr. David Daniels, the Basic Propositions are the most succinct and operational distillation of each Enneagram Type that exists. They describe each Enneagram Type from our most essential, wonderful qualities down to our most contracted, defensive, back-on-our-bullshit selves. In my time as

---

*David N. Daniels and Virginia A. Price, *The Essential Enneagram: The Definitive Personality Test and Self-Discovery Guide,* rev. ed. (New York: HarperOne, 2009).

an Enneagram practitioner, the Basic Propositions have been the best tool I've encountered to observe our patterns in real time, giving us the best possible chance at breaking them. In my not-so-humble opinion, our ego stands no chance in the boxing ring against the one-two punch that is a working knowledge of the Basic Proposition of our Type and a grounded sense of humor about ourselves. So, I submit my book to you as your boxing trainer, getting you to your fighting weight for the ten rounds of your life against yourself and your patterns.

Prior to understanding the Basic Propositions, or elements of them, I found the presentation of Type within this framework very intellectual and theoretical. But as I studied them more and particularly as I heard from people of each Type reflecting on how each element of the Basic Propositions manifested in their real lives, I came to see how the sequence of beliefs and fears would feed into predictable behavior, which improved the clarity of the Types, making the Enneagram much more practical.

So, in the hope of offering you the same brilliantly practical insights about each of the nine Types, here are the elements of the Basic Propositions that we'll cover.

ESSENTIAL STATE

The Essential State, or Essence, of each Type is the pure and unencumbered way that each Type came into the world and describes the best gifts that each Type has to offer. It isn't something we cultivate or strengthen. We are born with it, and when we are in an expanded, integrated place, we don't even have to work for it; it simply channels through us by our very presence. It's the gift that we are meant to give to this world with abundant generosity and ease. Sounds great, right? Not so fast, y'all. It's all downhill from here . . .

CORE BELIEF

Here's where it all starts to go wrong. No matter how wonderful and spectacular and loving our parents may be, there isn't a single soul walking this earth that grew up in a perfect environment. Our caregivers have their own wounds and trauma, and despite their best efforts, they impart those to us. (Hey, caregivers, it's okay. This isn't one of those "blame your caregivers" books. We know you did the best you could.) As a result of an imperfect holding environment, every person loses contact with their Essence, and as they observe an imperfect world around them, a fundamental and unconscious Core Belief begins to form about that imperfect world. It's important to note that, in Enneagram theory, our Core Belief is cemented in the very earliest part of our development—by the time we are three or four years of age. **The Core Belief of each Type articulates the distinct way that we perceive and understand the character of the world around us, and this Core Belief often isn't a particularly charitable worldview.** Sometimes referred to as the cognitive distortion, the Core Belief can be likened to the drunk goggles of our Type. In the same way that drunk goggles distort our vision and cause us to overcompensate as we navigate, our Core Belief distorts our perspective on the world, and our patterns of behavior are our attempt to stumble through the world as we see it.

CORE FEAR

Out of the Core Belief comes the Core Fear of each Type. If the world is *this particular way,* then I need to be on guard against *this particular thing.* **The Core Fear is the thing or things that each Type is working overtime to avoid at all costs,** and the Core Fear being triggered is what sets all our defensive strategies into motion, reproducing the greatest hits of our worst patterns.

FOCUS OF ATTENTION

As you can imagine, when you walk around trying to avoid something, it makes sense that you are on the lookout for the warning signs of the thing you're trying to avoid. This is the Focus of Attention of each Type. The Focus of Attention is what preoccupies the internal threat scanner of our minds. **The Focus of Attention is the evidence that each Type tends to look for in support of the conclusion we've already reached about how the world operates.**

IDEALIZED SELF-IMAGE

The Idealized Self-Image is the performance of self that we have constructed based on what we believe about the world and what we are afraid of. In short, **the Idealized Self-Image is who we believe we need to be in response to the very particular world we perceive around us and the threat that always looms.** We are *very* attached to this image of ourselves; we spend a lot of time and energy to project it into the world. In many ways, it's our core strategy for survival. And if we understand that it's our ego that creates a cheap imitation of our Essential State, the Idealized Self-Image is exactly that imitation in its everyday form.

DEFENSE MECHANISM

David Daniels understood the Defense Mechanism as the glue that holds the entire ego structure together.* **Our Defense Mechanism allows our Core Belief, Core Fear, and Idealized Self-Image to continue to feed into one another.** Each Type has a very particular Defense Mechanism, and knowing what that Defense

---

*David N. Daniels, "The Basic Proposition: The Foundation of Personality," drdaviddaniels.com/the-basic-propositions/.

Mechanism is helps us identify the Jenga piece that, when removed, will bring the whole tower to the ground.

VICE

The Vice of each Type, sometimes referred to as the Passion, can be better understood as the emotional experience of each Type when our Core Fear is triggered. **Our Vice both amplifies and further fuels the behavioral strategies we've adopted as survival tactics in stress.** In particular, our Vice is a pattern that reinforces our Idealized Self-Image. A fun little etymology lesson for my word nerds out there, specific to the use of the word *passion* and its place in the Enneagram ego structure: The late Latin source of *passion* is *passio,* which translates to "suffering." So our Vice, or Passion, is the very real emotional suffering we experience when we're at our worst.

VIRTUE

An antidote to our Vice, **our Virtue is our higher emotional state.** Unlike Essence, our Virtue must be cultivated through self-awareness and conscious pattern breaking. Our Virtue is our emotional experience of our Essence—it's openhearted, expanded, and expansive and an absolute affront to our carefully curated Idealized Self-Image.

While general Enneagram literature can be eerily accurate at describing our innermost gore, it goes without saying that we all also bring our own unique life experiences to our understanding of ourselves. The Basic Propositions and widely accepted Type descriptions can get us pretty far, but I would contend that there is immense value in figuring out how to articulate our Core Belief, Core Fear, and Idealized Self-Image in our own words.

The value of putting these key elements of the Basic Proposition of your Type into your own words is that they hit differently when you're speaking your own language. As an example, the Idealized Self-Image of the Eight, in most traditional Enneagram writing, is articulated as being strong and in control. Sure, that tracks for me: I like people to view me as strong and in control. But when I was able to put my own language to my Idealized Self-Image—that I want to be seen not just as strong or in control but as a pillar—it kind of kicked the door open for me in terms of transformational substance to unpack. What does it mean to me to be a pillar versus strong and in control? Well, pillars are often made of solid stone, usually some kind of marble. They are strong enough to support entire buildings, enormous amounts of weight resting on them at all hours of the day and night, and they tend to be pretty difficult to move. . . . Ya see how much more that reveals about who I think I have to be in my relationships, as opposed to just "strong and in control"?

While the Core Belief is the lens through which we perceive our experiences and thus colors how we view the world, I think the best way to find our own unique articulation of that Core Belief is actually by starting out with our Idealized Self-Image. As human beings, we tend to have an understanding of ourselves and the role we play more readily available on the surface of our consciousness. It's in expressing that personality that we can begin to uncover what we believe about the world and then what we're trying to avoid.

Idealized Self-Image

So, concretely, here are some questions we can ask ourselves to begin to put our own words to our Idealized Self-Image:

- Who do I think I have to be in my relationships?
- Who do I think I have to be to get my needs met?
- What role did I play in my family of origin?

- What role do I play in my current professional and personal environments?

Spend some time with those questions; spare no gory detail. The more vivid a picture you're able to paint of yourself, the more information you'll have about how you perceive the world and the threats that you're navigating around.

Core Belief

Now as this Idealized Self-Image begins to take shape and come together, this is where you're going to start digging a little bit deeper. The questions here aren't particularly complex, but you can certainly keep asking yourself the same question over and over again to get to deeper layers of your Core Belief:

- Why do I believe I have to be [fill in the blank with your Idealized Self-Image]?
- How did I come to believe I had to be [Idealized Self-Image]?
- Which of my needs are met when I play the role of [Idealized Self-Image]?
- What evidence do I have that I have to be [Idealized Self-Image]?

Can you see how, now that we've got your Idealized Self-Image expressed more clearly, the rest of the landscape also starts to fill in? These questions are going to reveal what kind of blanket statements you perceive to be fundamentally true about the world. And as you begin to understand and put your own words to how you perceive the world, the scary monster that lurks in that world is also going to begin to emerge in sharper focus.

Core Fear

This isn't the time to lean out, all right? I know we're getting a little bit dark here, but the Core Fear is the domino that falls first and knocks everything else down. And having your own specific, precise language for it will help you catch it in real time in a way that the generic Enneagram write-ups might not. So, put on your big-kid pants and keep digging. Here are some questions to get at your Core Fear:

- If I don't get my needs met, what might happen?
- If I stop performing this role for my loved ones, what might happen?
- What is at risk if I stop protecting myself by being [Idealized Self-Image]?

I know, it's spooky stuff. But *this* is the real magic of the Enneagram. It puts concrete, clear language to the things we're already scared of. It names the world we think we operate in and the strategy we adopt just to get through the day so that we can understand our patterns as a protective strategy and not confuse them with our true identity. Once you understand the mechanisms of the ego structure, you stop identifying so much with it and are no longer completely subject to it. It takes time, it takes practice, and our ego structure is almost always at least one step ahead of us. But when we know what we're looking for, we have so much more capacity to interrupt the well-worn patterns of self-protection that actually impede our fulfillment in life.

In addition to a dive into the Basic Proposition of each Type, each chapter will look at frequent patterns and relational struggles of each Type (also known as the ways in which each Type is a massive pain in the butt to the people around them), because none of us are actually that special or unique (sorry, Fours). Unflattering though they are, these common Type-specific stumbling blocks will give us a clearer illustration of how the elements of the Basic Proposition are interacting within us in our moments of stress, thus perpetuating these familiar problems.

If you're the kindhearted, dutiful reader who is reading this introduction and indeed this entire book in the order it was written, then you're going to notice that there's a degree of redundancy in each chapter as I explain the Basic Proposition of each Type. Let me assure you, that's by design and not a sign of you slowly losing your marbles. There may be other signs of your deteriorating grasp on reality, but the repetitive rhythm of each chapter isn't one of them.

As I learned long ago, most people love it when they're the center of the conversation, so in an effort to correct for the fact that many will skip right over this well-written and thoughtful explanation of the framework of each Type, I re-explain myself in each chapter with the benefit of concrete examples and Type-specific context. Anyway, I just wanted to write a note to my good students to say, you're not losing it. Each chapter *is* reiterative, because some people just wanna read about themselves, and if we're being honest, those are the people who probably most need to gain a clear understanding of themselves.

DISCLAIMER

Many years ago, a well-intentioned but misunderstanding teacher told me that they considered what I was doing with the Enneagram as "borderline sacrilegious," and they couldn't wrap their mind around the idea that holding yourself accountable could go hand in hand with having a sense of humor about yourself. But if I've learned anything in my life, it's that humor can take the bite out of the things about us that are otherwise too difficult to confront. With my whole being, I believe there is great spiritual wisdom in levity; if we can laugh at something, we can look at it and, eventually, we can learn from it. **My hope is that, within these pages, you'll find some practical strategies for liberating yourself from yourself and your defensive postures while being empowered to laugh at yourself in the process.** And if I can be *particularly* greedy with my hopes for you at the conclusion of this book (taking a cue from Type Sevens), **my ultimate dream for you is that you'll not only be able to stop yourself from sliding back into an unconscious, autopilot protective mode but also be able to extend grace and compassion to those protective behaviors that did indeed keep you safe and serve you at various points in your life.** Because it's this self-compassion that ultimately translates into the kind of outwardly directed compassion that creates space for healing to happen and confidence to grow. The kind of compassion that overflows out of us and onto the rest of the world. The world is heavy enough, and so is the work of growth and healing. But that doesn't mean we can't find both reprieve and strength in the lighthearted and outrageous. Humor can be more than just a doorway; it can be the very path by which we journey even deeper into the work.

ETHICAL ETIQUETTE OF
THE ENNEAGRAM AND OTHER
HOUSEKEEPING ITEMS

I've got to warn you, friends. This last section will be brief, but it will be a bit of a buzzkill. There are a lot of shenanigans going on out there in the Wild West that is the Enneagram corner of the internet, and we have to talk about it. I'm not gonna write an entire book about the Enneagram and then let you loose into the world to be an absolute turkey about it, like a second-semester freshman hot off their first introduction to Nietzsche, insufferable in their newfound nihilism.

I tend to reject the title of Enneagram Expert whenever it is thrust upon me, because (1) it's a bit stuffy for me and (2) I see myself as more of the class clown than the expert in the room. That said, I still think there are some guiding principles that any Enneagram practitioner, teacher, fellow class clown, or general enthusiast worth their salt should adhere to. And I earnestly believe that if we all honored them, we'd have a better Enneagram world.

ETHICAL ETIQUETTE

First, foremost, and for the love of all that is good and spicy, **do not diagnose anyone with a Type.** I don't care if they're your best friend, your lover, your mother, or your kid, I don't care if you think they're wrong about their Type, and I don't care how many Enneagram books you've read and workshops you've attended. If you haven't been specifically trained to conduct typing interviews, you aren't qualified to type someone else. This is, admittedly, the most buzzkill-ish of the buzzkills in this section, but it's also probably the most important. I know, as far as temptations go, typing someone is up there with cheesecake, which is to say, incredibly, painfully tempting.

Despite how much I do truly enjoy being a bully and telling you what to do, there are actually some very valid reasons you should resist the urge to type others. Above all, typing someone else is interfering with their unique journey of arriving at their Type. **Coming to land on our Type is a deeply personal experience, and it requires the practice of self-honesty and self-awareness, which isn't something you can do for someone else.**

Which brings me to another reason we can't possibly type someone else. **All we can really observe is behavior, which is absolutely *not* the basis of Type.** If we're lucky, friends may share their inner world with us, and if that's the case, we can certainly accompany them on their journey to find their Type, but we still aren't in charge of deciding when their destination has been reached.

Last, and this is an important one, we're human beings that have, over the course of our lifetimes, absorbed unconscious messages about certain identities that we hold—gender, race, sexuality, religion—and they come along with some pretty loaded cultural tropes. Even the most intentional among us, who are doing the work to unpack our unconscious biases, will always have plenty of baggage left to unpack. And those unconsciously held beliefs about certain people based on their identity will inevitably interfere with our assessment of them. As an example, there are an extraordinary number of women (your beloved author included!) who identify as a Two (Nurturer) or a Nine (Peacemaker) when they first encounter the Enneagram. It's only after unpacking the messaging they've received about how they were supposed to be self-sacrificial or play the peacemaker role in their family of origin that they realize, *Wait. I'm conflating these cultural values around the "right" way to be femi-nine with Type.* Similarly, if my Bumble career has shown me anything, a lot of straight men seem to see themselves reflected in the Three (Performer), Five (Investigator), or Eight (Challenger/Protector). Some of them may indeed be Threes, Fives, and Eights, but some of them may just be confusing the overlap between the Type descriptions and socially constructed standards about what is masculine. It's bad enough when we do this to ourselves; it's far worse when we project our unconscious biases onto others.

As tempting as it is, be the bigger person and don't fall victim to the siren song of projecting your Type assumptions onto someone else. Let them have their journey, and you focus on yours. Speaking of which, **your journey is decidedly *not* going to involve using your Type as an excuse to be an unapologetic menace.** Giving ourselves a hall pass to be a jerk just because we finally have the language to describe what we're afraid of is the same thing as going to a few therapy sessions and then using the terms you learned to be even more toxic.

People don't always understand that there is a whole function to the Enneagram. It's not just a cutesy little description that can be summed up in an aesthetic Canva JPEG, nor is it a life sentence. It's meant to shed a very clear light on our worst behavior precisely so that we can catch ourselves in real time when our patterns start patterning. Excusing a lack of boundaries because you're a Two or writing off your emotional stinginess because you're a Five isn't what the Enneagram is here for, so knock it off!

In a similar vein . . . **it's equally poor form for you to write someone off entirely because of *their* Type.** It's almost inevitable that, over the course of a casual conversation about the Enneagram, someone will start the trash-talking, and soon enough, everyone is pleading their case, complete with evidence and closing arguments, about why their least favorite Type is the actual worst Type on the Enneagram. Sometimes people ask me if there are sort of natural enemies among the Types—oil-and-water Types that are naturally inclined to dislike each other. As an example, Sevens (Adventurers) and Ones (Perfectionists) often get pitted against each other, but they also often get married, so your guess is as good as mine on that pairing. Anyway, no, I don't think it's necessarily the case that certain Types are fated to dislike each other. And I don't care how good your rationale is for your dislike of a certain Type—it can almost always be boiled down to something within yourself, instead of the structure of that Type.

When we have a reaction to a Type Two (Nurturer), or all Type Twos, it's because they're reflecting something back to us that we haven't integrated within ourselves. Either we haven't given ourselves permission or we haven't given ourselves compassion for the very same thing that we're raging against in the Two. When I, as an Eight (Challenger), roll my eyes at the emotional sensitivity of a Four (Romantic), it has less to do with the Four and a lot more to do with the fact that I have so buried my vulnerability that it takes the force of an earthquake to move me affectively and remind me of my sensitivity. When I get annoyed at Sevens for their lack of focus, it's less about the actual task that isn't getting done or the Seven who isn't following through and more about the resentment I feel at the way I haven't given myself permission to let someone else take on some of the heavy burden of the work. Annoyance at another Type is an invitation for us to get curious about what we haven't permitted within ourselves and is all the more reason that it's rude *and* unhelpful to write off an entire Type because they're getting on our nerves.

I know I already said that not typing someone else was the most important of rules to adhere to when sharing the Enneagram, but as an Eight, rules are mere suggestions to me, even the ones I make up on my own, so there's another equally important rule when it comes to ethical practice of the Enneagram. **Remember that none of our patterns developed in a vacuum.** We didn't come up with these obnoxious strategies for survival just for the hell of it. All the self-sabotaging patterns that we cycle back to have kept us safe and helped us get our needs met. The reason this reminder is so important is that once we start to recognize the impact of our defensive actions on ourselves and on others, it can be easy to start feeling crappy about them. From there, the shame spiral can consume us pretty quickly. This humiliation can cause us to resign ourselves to our patterns, rather than recognizing that—now that we know what's going on—we have agency to hold ourselves accountable for doing better. Remembering that these patterns actually do serve a very practical function can help us ward off some of that shame and invite a little compassion for the version of ourselves that didn't know any better.

HOUSEKEEPING ITEMS

Many Enneagram books talk about the dynamism of the Enneagram—specifically, wings and stress and security points— and to be clear, these are important elements to become familiar with. Wings are the Types to either side of your dominant Type, and while most people have a more dominant wing, we all have both wings available to us. Stress and security points, which are sometimes called integration and disintegration points, refer to a Type's tendency to take on the characteristics of another Type when they're healthy or stressed.

Perhaps this is a controversial stance, but I think that people tend to turn wings and stress points into convenient scapegoats for our bad behavior. Rather than interrogating our own motivations and starting from the place of acknowledging that if we're out of pocket, it's because the Core Fear of our Type is triggered, we point to our stress Type and claim that's the source of our acting out. Not only is that common discourse a total misunderstanding of how the dynamism of the Enneagram works, but it's also focusing on the *symptoms* of our fear rather than the *root cause* of it.

With that said . . . what I *will* say about wings and stress and security points is that they point to the fact that we have access to all nine Types. We're not actually locked into only one way of operating. Wings and stress and security points, much like the quirks that annoy us about other Types, are all invitations to break our patterns and try to entertain another perspective as though it were as valid as our own—because it is! Accessing another perspective allows us to take it seriously and extend compassion to the person who naturally operates from that perspective. And that is all the airtime I'm going to dedicate to wings and stress and security points in this book.

As a final housekeeping note, you'll notice as you make your way through this book that I often use the phrase *ego structure* or simply *ego*. For the sake of clarity, it's important that you know I'm not using it in the Freudian sense. *Ego* or *ego structure*, when I discuss the Enneagram, is just another term for the personality we built to protect ourselves, not some part of our consciousness that's responding to some other part.

Okay, housekeeping items are officially done, and you made it through the biggest bummer of a chapter in the whole book: the rules. Now we can get into the good stuff!

Part II

THE GUT CENTER

INTRODUCTION TO THE GUT CENTER

Perhaps the strangest of bedfellows, or gut fellows, as the case is, Types Eight, Nine, and One make up the triad known as the Gut Center. These big, bad, bold Types, at first blush, can look pretty markedly different: Eights are something between a wrecking ball and a bulldozer, demolishing anything in their way and delighting in flagrantly disregarding the rules. Nines are chill, go with the flow, seemingly lacking in energy, and, in contrast to Eights and Ones, generally well liked. Ones are principled, rigid, and unforgiving—often as obviously pissed off as Eights but not nearly as willing to openly express it.

The Gut Center of the Enneagram contains people who experience the world through their bodies. Their energy is often visceral, not only to themselves but also to the people around them. You can feel them in the room before you see them, and honestly, sometimes their energy is so big that they give off vibes just by being in the general vicinity, like a disturbance in the Force. The Gut Center is a juicy bunch of Types, with an abundance of strength and energy. They're the kick in the keister that the whole Enneagram system needs among all the emotional angst and intellectual anxiety of the other two Centers.

Here are some things that come naturally to the Gut Center Types:

- a focus on the immediate and present
- an intense strength and stamina

- a fierce and defiant expression of their stubborn self-determination and agency
- a ferocious defense system around their boundaries, sometimes (often) at the expense of the boundaries of others

These aren't Types that long for the past or wring their hands about the future; these are Types that are right *here* and right *now*. The benefit of this orientation toward the present moment is that they are indeed present to those around them. And when they're in the moment in a relaxed, undefended way, they can spring into action with an innate, somatic wisdom that empowers and grounds those around them. The downside to this immediate attention is that if it's not on their radar right now, Eights, Nines, and Ones are likely to forget or procrastinate on it. It also means that the thing they're focused on in the present is subject to the intense spotlight of the Gut Center Types' attention. Talk about a hot seat.

Eights' immediate attention generally results in immediate action. Eights shoot first, aim later. Nines' attention is often on the vibes: Is everyone cool, or is the possibility of conflict breathing down our necks, threatening to upend the chill mood? Ones' attention lands on what is incorrect within the environment and what opportunities they have to flex their moral superiority.

The source of Gut Center Types' ability to empower others is their impressive, somatically generated strength. The obvious and rock-solid power that the Eight embodies is not only in their ability to support others, but also in a heart that is strong enough to risk vulnerability. The grounded, steady strength of the Nine is a force of reconciliation and repair, bringing broken pieces back together. The reliable and structurally sound strength of the One provides the scaffolding and integrity required for reform.

However, this somatic strength is also the source of a lot of the Gut Center's garbage. The strength of the Eight supports them in their intimidation tactics. The strength of the Nine enables them to effectively numb themselves to the world. The strength of the One allows them to keep on going well past the point of exhaustion so that they can appear selfless and responsible, rather than just taking a break.

While Eights may be the loudest and most obnoxious about their commitment to self-determination and autonomy, forging their own path on their own terms is a hallmark of all the Gut Center Types. Many Eights report that, as early as childhood, they bucked rules and constraints, constantly ending up in a battle of wills with their caregivers and any authority figure. Nines take a softer, although no less strong, stance in their stubborn self-determination, opting to avoid anything they don't want to do by passive resistance: showing up late, if they don't sleep through the thing entirely. They don't make the same scene that Eights do, but you still aren't winning this round. Ones' willful expression of their autonomy is in their strict adherence to and insistence on their self-authored standards, convinced that if everyone just did things their way, the world would be a better place (jury is still out on that, Ones).

Boundaries are another big theme for Eights, Nines, and Ones. They're intensely defensive of their own and maddeningly dismissive of the boundaries of others. The enforcement of boundaries for Gut Center Types boils down to the issue of control. Eights defend their boundaries by bullying and pushing the boundaries of others, provoking and pushing others until they push back. Nines protect their boundaries by disengaging from the present moment and the present conflict and disregard the boundaries of others by simply merging into the dreams, desires, and priorities of others until they can no longer distinguish them from their own. Ones enforce their boundaries by adhering to strict standards of goodness and by making themselves so busy that they don't have space or time for anything else. They disrespect the boundaries of others by imposing their stringent, near-impossible standards on them and judging them mercilessly for missing the mark.

The other thing that these three Types have in common? A

marked relationship with anger. Eights, Nines, and Ones orient to anger very distinctly from one another, but the fact remains that anger is the sun around which each of these planets orbit. The most obvious member of the Anger Triad is the Eight, openly belligerent and delighting in hand-to-hand combat for sport. The Eight is also the most obvious example of the concept of anger being a protective, secondary emotion: Open, unabashed anger serves them in that it creates a terrifying force field around their vulnerability, warding off anyone who might come too close to the more tender aspects of their experience.

The Nine, in contrast, is probably the most confusing member of the anger cohort. Even their archetypal name, the Peacemaker, conflicts with their place in the Anger Triad. The Nine is the most disconnected from their anger, deep asleep to all their self-abandonment and self-betrayal. They rarely recognize their anger and, as a result, can't predict the innocuous thing that is going to light the fuse on all that buried rage. Nines report that their anger is often sloppy and comes out sideways; when it erupts, the spark that sets it off isn't necessarily the thing that they're actually angry about.

Last, the One is in a wrestling match with their anger, constantly trying to pin it to the mat, lest it come out, ugly and uncontrolled. Anger is a frustrating double bind for the One: It feels so deliciously self-righteous when it flares up, and at the same time, they stubbornly refuse to give it full-throated expression. Anger can be messy, irrational, and destructive, which is exactly why the One works so hard to control it. The moral superiority they feel when they successfully swallow their rage is *almost* worth all the work.

Perhaps at the tender heart of all this anger in the Gut Triad is the pattern of self-forgetting that all three Types unconsciously engage in. Eights forget their innocence, vulnerability, and interdependence and instead arm themselves with crust and crass, resulting in anger at their inability to relax and let someone else take the wheel in their relationships. Nines forget their own significance, merging with others, latching on to their relationships at the expense of their dreams and values, even values as inconsequential as a preference for chunky peanut butter over smooth. Ones forget that they're allowed to be human, to mess up, to get it wrong and then learn and grow. Instead, they hold themselves to the impossible standard of perfection, beating themselves up for missing an impossible mark.

While Eights, Nines, and Ones are remarkably different Types with different motivations and patterns, they're bound by many of the same strengths and much of the same suffering. Spending most of their time roiling in anger and playing goalie in defense of their agency, these three Types are three different embodiments of the Strong One™. Remarkable in their ability to support and inspire others in turning their thoughts and emotions into action, Eights, Nines, and Ones are at their best when they remember their tenderness, their significance, and their humanity as the very source of their agency and strength.

TYPE EIGHT

Large, in Charge, and Just *This Side of Belligerent*

It's incredibly difficult not to start this chapter with a long string of expletives, because naughty four-letter words are the love language of the Enneagram's resident rebel, the Type Eight. It's difficult for me not to start out with a long string of cusswords precisely *because* I'm an Eight and I'm writing to my people. But for the sake of the folks who love us, who aren't fluent in how swear words can be terms of endearment, and who are just trying to gain deeper understanding of who we are and how to access our well-protected but marshmallow-squishy hearts, I will grudgingly (and heavily) rely on the thesaurus to translate my beloved obscenity into more socially acceptable prose.

As has been just stated above and is fairly evident based on absolutely everything about me, I'm an Eight and I love Eights. I think we're awesome, but I'm going to do my best to be just as unrelenting to my own Type as I am to every other Type. Fair is fair, and it's a bit of an understatement to say that Eights can be bullies, cranking up the volume on their naturally big energy to intimidate others and instigating arguments for sport, fighting with as much intensity over pizza toppings as they do over issues of injustice. In *The Essential Enneagram*, David Daniels writes this about how Eights think: "I may not win every battle with others, but they'll know I've been there."*

Intimidating whether they intend to be or not, Eights often really like that they have a reputation for being formidable and will

---

*Daniels and Price, *The Essential Enneagram*, 5.

happily lean into it when it serves their best interests. Their bark and accompanying and proportionately matched bite are their bid for dominance over their environment. Whether it's theirs to take or not, Eights commandeer control over their environment by demonstrations of rebellion, delightedly disrespecting any prospective foes and displaying open hostility toward any perceived constraints on their agency.

The Challenger and the Protector, the archetypal names of the Eight, bring to mind images of a noble warrior, steeled by an inner courage and a willingness to make the ultimate sacrifice for the ones they've chosen to defend. That's a nice thought, but the reality is a lot less virtuous and a lot more belligerent. In practice, the Eight is more warthog than warrior. There's a description of the warthog on the Animal in You website that could double as a summary of the Eight: "Neither polished nor good-looking, warthogs have stumbled upon a unique combination of aggression and charisma and have adopted it as their survival strategy."*

Aside from the fact that we're devastatingly sexy as a whole, that description does track for Protectors when we're behaving badly. Shooting first and taking aim later (if at all), Eights are people of instinct and immediate action. And honestly, their instincts are usually pretty good, so you can't really blame them for having such unapologetic confidence. The trouble comes when Challengers decide that their good instincts are the same as immutable, capital-T Truth and, in their efforts to defend it, they get rowdy and rude, daring anyone to question them.

To the non-Eight reading this chapter, it may seem that I'm being particularly rough with my Protector siblings, but with Eights, you're going to lose them real quick if you start with all the flattery. They see right through it. Eights respond much better to a hot roast right out of the gate so that they can trust you to be honest with them. Then, and only then, can you make them

---

*"The Warthog Personality," The Animal in You, animalinyou.com/animals/warthog.

squirm by naming all the positive attributes of this crusty Type. With that said, don't you think it's about time to make some Eights squirm?

Despite how most of us experience Eights, and even how Eights experience Eights, the Protector is perhaps the most tenderhearted Type on the Enneagram. They just have a very abrasive, rough shell encasing that tender heart, which is then surrounded by an alligator-infested moat, which is then guarded by a fire-breathing dragon with the bad attitude of a teenager with embarrassing parents. But even if you never catch a glimpse of the soft, sensitive core of the Eight, you've still probably felt the strength of their support, the solid security of their protectiveness, and the stability of their self-confidence. Unhampered by a fear of failure, the Eight prefers trial and error to meticulous planning, self-assured in their ability to navigate without much preparation and trusting in the reliability of their off-the-cuff game. Much like the Type Three, a healthy Eight is like a battery that instantly charges up the entire room. Their energy is huge, and they have an ease in the spotlight, with both a groundedness that commands the room and an electric intensity that leaves everyone with a little bit of a buzz.*

The best evidence of that sweet and tender heart hiding under the prickly rind of the Eight is their **Essential State.** Theirs is **an innocent approach to each person and the world at large that senses truth deep in everyone and everything.** Often referred to as empowerment, the Eight's inner strength is so steady that it provides others with both the support and the confidence to contact their own inner reserves of strength and faith in themselves. The Eight has a truly generous heart, especially for the vulnerable, and a truly iron backbone to stand up against abuses of power. Speaking of which, their heart is often described as magnanimous—they have the courage and lavish capacity to forgive. *Record scratch.* Wait. Did I just say "lavish capacity to forgive"? No, dear reader, you

---

*brb, going to copy and paste that into my Bumble profile . . .

didn't bump your head and somehow end up in a different chapter; you're still reading about the Eight. In fairness, the Challenger isn't exactly famous for being particularly forgiving of offenses. Quite the opposite—they often take it on themselves to even the score, whether it's on their own behalf or on behalf of someone else they believe has been wronged.

The disconnect between Eights' capacity to forgive and their practice of getting even begins with their **Core Belief.** They believe that **the people who hold power in the world wield their influence with cruelty, exploiting and exercising control over those who have any vulnerability exposed.** You know what? The Eights aren't wrong. But before you get too cocky, Eights, let me remind you that the Core Belief of *every* Type rings true; you're not special. But back to my point: We do live in a world that can feel awfully dog-eat-dog, and the powerful are happy to bend and outright break the rules for their own benefit, regardless of who ends up bearing the cost. Eights see a world that wants to take away their agency by exploiting their vulnerabilities, and from that grim perspective, they steel themselves against any son of a biscuit who would try them.

> *Eights see a world that wants to take away their agency by exploiting their vulnerabilities.*

Whether the authority they're sizing up is someone with some kind of institutional power, like a boss or a politician, or someone with relational power, like a parent or a partner, Eights have an automatic orientation of "fork around and find out" toward the person who is designated as in charge. It's less that Challengers need to be in control and more that they need the person in control to recognize that they won't be controlled. But in their ferocious defense of their own agency, Eights end up seizing control from everyone else and monster-truck-rallying all over everyone in the arena, becoming the very domineering force that they're trying to avoid falling prey to.

In their search for confirmation of the belief they already hold as capital-T Truth, Eights' **Focus of Attention** is **egregious injustices and abuses of power by those in charge.** Looking for a Goliath to go David on, Eights find fault with anyone who seems too eager to take the lead, sniffing out all their inconsistencies with as much social grace and subtlety as a toddler sneezing. They enter anything they find into evidence in a trial of trustworthiness. Unfortunately for the unsuspecting defendant in this civil case, their innocence isn't presumed, regardless of the evidence. Eights work backward, starting the trial by subjecting their opponent to a brutal sentence because they've already handed down a guilty verdict.

As is probably abundantly clear by now, the **Core Fear** of this generally fearless Type is **the exposure of their vulnerability leading to the loss of their autonomy.** Essentially, they fear that people who have access to their vulnerability will use it to betray them, effectively taking away their ability to chart their own course and self-define. Underneath all their bluster and spiky façade, Eights are acutely aware of the tenderness and sensitivity that reside within them, and they worry that their buried gentle nature is the Achilles' heel that will take them down when discovered. And when they look around and see how many warm and receptive people are taken advantage of and manipulated by some selfish dingleberry, it makes sense that they would fear for their own sweet little hearts and their capacity for self-determination.

For all of us, the activation of the Core Fear is the event that kick-starts our ego structure into motion, producing and reproducing our self-sabotaging cycles over and over again, despite what we claim we want. So, when Eights feel that their autonomy is being threatened, it sets off a whole chain reaction, giving us the patterns of belligerence and combativeness that make up most Type Eight descriptions.

By projecting a tough, secure, and decisive persona, they're scaring off and thus filtering out the people too spineless to be relied on.

Afraid that they'll be subject to someone else's whim, the Eight forges an **Idealized**

Self-Image that is **part human, part machine, and all menace.** They put forth a persona that is stronger than a roided-out Cross-Fit gym owner—hyper-independent, quick with a controversial opinion, and as ungovernable as the five potty-mouthed African gray parrots at a British zoo that had to be separated because they kept swearing at people when they were together.* The Eight's Idealized Self-Image makes such a scene by being brash and abrasive that even if people did want to try to control them, they'd have to think twice about whether or not it would be worth the trouble. The internal logic for the Eight here is that by projecting a tough, secure, and decisive persona, they're scaring off and thus filtering out the people too spineless to be relied on and trusted with their secret inner sensitivity.

Eights often position themselves as the protective provider in their relationships.

I'm being a bit harsh for comedic effect—because the Eights can take it. But what's helpful to keep in mind is that the Idealized Self-Image is a cheap reproduction of the best of each Type. So, tracking the difference between our unique gift and the off-brand version of it is important if we're trying to catch ourselves in our self-defeating patterns in real time. Equally important to remember, particularly as we look at the Idealized Self-Image, is that this element of our ego structure is not just a self-image but a strategy that *has* kept us safe and helped us get our needs met. A prime example of this is how Eights often position themselves as the protective provider in their relationships, not only as a way to feel strong but also as an incredibly convenient way to avoid acknowledging the support and protection that they also need in their relationships.

As we've previously covered, the Essence of the Eight is a strong presence that empowers and a courageous heart that forgives. The

*Sophie Lewis, "Five Parrots Separated at British Zoo After Encouraging Each Other to Curse Profusely at Guests," CBS News, cbsnews.com/news/parrots-separated-england-zoo-cursing-swearing-at-guests.

strength of the Challenger is not in their enormous energy or stamina, nor in the accuracy of their instincts when they're in charge, nor even in the fearlessness with which they lead others. It's in the way their support helps ground other people in their own strength and stability. Likewise, the magnanimous heart of the Eight doesn't forgive out of moral superiority—for the sake of being the bigger person. But it risks the vulnerability of being hurt again, recognizing that the relationship is ultimately too important to remain in conflict with the other person. The Eight is most powerful when they give their strength away, helping other people recognize their agency and giving them freedom from their past mistakes in the form of forgiveness.

The bargain-basement version of that incredible (and, may I say, incredibly sexy) Essence is the brutish strength and unbridled intensity that enter the room five minutes before the Eight does. Seizing the reins without regard for social niceties and previously established hierarchies, the Idealized Self-Image is entirely committed to gaining and maintaining control. The Eight muscles through life like they're running an *American Ninja Warrior* obstacle course. Bucking even the slightest resistance with the most belligerent forcefulness, the Challenger approaches everything as though it requires a struggle of both will and might. If ego is an imitation of Essence, the Idealized Self-Image of the Eight is, at best, a terrible impression of the powerful matter of their Essence.

It's not just important but actually essential to pause here and acknowledge that none of our bad behaviors and out-of-pocket patterns developed in a vacuum. Eights have been able to get their needs met, keep themselves safe, and even earn love and admiration by donning the mask of their Idealized Self-Image. Eights are trusted with leadership because of their comfort with taking the wheel. Their belligerence and rowdiness have been a formidable defense against those threatening to take away their autonomy. And indeed, Eights are loved and admired for their fearless championing of the vulnerable and their bold and direct speaking of truth to power. I know I've been dogging on the Idealized Self-Image for being a cheap version of the real thing, but it's important to remember that however cheap it is, the front that anyone puts forward is effective and has been their means of survival in dire moments. So, while I want you to ultimately be free of this façade, I remind you of how useful it has been so that you can remember to extend some compassion to yourself for relying on it for so long.

Hey, non-Eights, can you hear that growl of discontent in the distance? The Eights are getting itchy again with all this soft "forgive yourself" talk and are threatening mutiny if I don't get back to roasting them, so we'd better return to the task at hand.

Denial, in the ferocious Challenger, shows up as a knee-jerk, visceral reaction of rejecting their own softness before anyone else has a chance to witness it.

The **Defense Mechanism** that keeps this whole beast snarling is denial—**denial of their vulnerability, denial of their limits and limitations, denial of their tenderness, denial of very real threats to their well-being, and denial of their interdependence and need for support.** Denial, in the ferocious Challenger, shows up as a knee-jerk, visceral reaction of rejecting their own softness before anyone else has a chance to witness it. In doing so, they *think* they are escaping the exploitation that awaits them if they let their guard down.

Denial supports the ego structure of the Eight in two key ways. First, by giving their vulnerability the cold shoulder, they can appear self-assured and decisive, even when they're not, allowing them to remain in control of themselves and out from under the influence, agenda, and determination of anyone else. Second, denial confirms what they believe about their vulnerability, specifically that it is a liability. By refusing to allow it to be witnessed and held with great care by other people, they deny themselves the opportunity to receive support and experience the connection that is often forged when vulnerability is given fresh air to breathe.

Lust goads Protectors into taking stupid risks and ramping up the intensity of simple disagreements.

The **Vice, or Passion,** is the emotional experience of each Type when they're knee deep in their patterns, and for Eights, that experience is known as lust. But before you get too excited, Protectors, I need you to know it's not the fun and sexy kind of lust. Lust, in the context of Eights' ego structure, is a **lust for intensity.** It's the rush of adrenaline that rises within them when they say something out of pocket or the thrill that they feel when they blatantly and gleefully break a rule or disrespect a social norm. Lust goads Protectors into taking stupid risks and ramping up the intensity of simple disagreements into a full-contact sport, all so they can feel ungovernable. The surge of intensity that floods them in a visceral way is both the byproduct and the fuel of their ego structure, making them feel alive and electrified, defiant and strong, prepared to enter any conversation or interaction like they're charging into an important battle.

As exciting and badass as that lust sounds, dear Eights, it takes a toll over the long term. We know that elevated levels of stress hormones such as adrenaline, over extended periods of time, raise our baseline for what our bodies consider normal. When our system stays flooded and activated, that fight-or-fight mechanism (Eights don't have much of a flight instinct) remains at the ready at all times. Essentially, we construct our own hair trigger. Paired with our Defense Mechanism, denial, which keeps us willfully rejecting our limitations and refusing to entertain the possibility that something could harm us, lust keeps us pushing the limits further and further, revving the engine until it finally goes up in flames hot enough to make the devil sweat. Look, I didn't think we'd get into a whole thing about our bodies' responses to intensity, but burnout is a very real and, in fact, very common occurrence for Eights that stay buck wild.

Not only the outcome and propellant of their ego structure, lust is also the response that the Challenger's personality offers to their anger. Anger is immediate for all the Gut Center Types, and the Eight's anger is often laser focused on perceived hostile-takeover attempts of their autonomy. Far be it for the Eight to back down from anything—their lust for intensity escalates what was very likely an honest misunderstanding into a full-blown conflict. They stare down the poor fool like they're a matador's waving red cape, letting the rising tension amplify their impending and inevitable charge, the buildup of intensity almost as brutalizing as the eventual gore itself.

By virtue of their reputation for being bullies, a lot has already been written about how Eights are difficult to be in relationship with, and you know what? We are. I'm not even going to bother arguing with that. In our attempt to get close to people, we put them through a series of tests that aren't for the faint of heart. I could defend us by pointing back to the sensitive lil heart that we're trying to protect, but I'm not here to write a chapter full of Type Eight apologetics, especially when we have a lot of (emotional) blood on our hands. Yes, we're trying to protect ourselves, but so is every other Type, and they don't resort to the guerilla warfare tactics that we employ, so that excuse doesn't really hold water. Instead of risking the vulnerability that we know genuine connection requires, Eights stiff-arm people's attempts at closeness, rejecting them before we get rejected. We test people by getting rowdy and staging conflict as a litmus test of others' trustworthiness, challenging anyone with any level of authority, regarding them with automatic contempt until they've proved themselves.

Eights are the living, breathing embodiment of the old saying "You can't fire me; I quit, [insert colorful insult of your choice]." Sensitive to being rejected but even more sensitive to being seen as sensitive, Eights anticipate rejection. They try to get out in front of it by firing off their own rebuff before the other person has even thought to draw their weapon. While it's clear to any casual observer that this pattern of rejecting before they're rejected is a protective measure, Eights can be pretty offensive in their self-defense. When they sense that someone might be able to inflict harm, their efforts veer into overkill, and they use brutality as their boundary, with little regard for the collateral damage of their preemptive strike. My fellow Eights, this knee-jerk stiff-arm move is one of the principal reasons our Type is frustratingly misunderstood and reduced to this one-dimensional eighties rom-com jock-bully prototype.* What would it be like for us to trust in the remarkable athleticism and might of our tender hearts instead of relying on our quick-draw rejection muscles?

One of the hallmarks of the Eight is their comfort—nay, *delight*—in conflict. Whereas many people do their best to avoid open conflict, the Protector seeks it out, stirring it up where it doesn't exist when they're bored. Engaging in a good scuffle scratches multiple itches for the Eight. Sometimes a verbal grapple wakes them up and makes them feel alive, and other times they engage in a cage match in order to provoke the other person into showing the true contents of their character when the gloves are off, a brutal test of trustworthiness. It's crucial to know that the Eight doesn't need you to agree with them in a conflict. In fact, yielding to the amped-up Protector too quickly may sabotage your attempts to earn their trust. They actually respect you more when you can stand up to them. The thinking is, if you can withstand the Eight's ferocious energy, then they can trust you when faced with something more sinister and hostile.

Lest it seem that I'm defending Eights for the nonchalant way they engineer conflict as a shortcut to trust building, let me call them out for what they're actually doing. By forcing people down the path of conflict in order to establish intimacy and faith, Eights are still demanding to be known by their might and not their more tender and gentle core. They're still refusing to allow people to fully see them, and in contrast to their typical pattern of

*See Stan Gable, Biff Tannen, and the Heathers.

rejecting others, in this instance, they're rejecting themselves before anyone else can. Challengers, I'm going to challenge you here to reflect on what you're so afraid of letting people see in you that you would prefer they see your big teeth and fighting chops instead. And what do you think you're protecting within yourself by trying to bypass a slower, steadier trust-building process?

Another nickname for the Eight that you'll occasionally see floating around Enneagram literature is the Boss. It's a fairly straightforward title that communicates their tendency to take charge, appointing themselves the team lead, whether it's appropriate or not. The Eight, having little interest in the quality or appearance of the outcome and, frankly, not giving a shit how their hostile takeover is received by anyone else, takes charge to avoid being subject to anyone else's agenda. They don't want to be governed by the values and rules of someone else, and it'll be a cold day in hell before they just surrender to someone else's lead without ensuring that they're in capable hands. Without realizing that they've put someone in the unfortunate posture of being on the defense, the Eight runs the prospective leader through any number of trials of integrity. The absurdity of this common scenario is that even if the Eight accepts someone else as a competent leader that they can get behind, they've still positioned themselves as the gatekeeper of acceptable leadership, granting themselves more power as they establish themselves as higher up in the hierarchy of whatever relational structure and situation this is. Which, of course, is the perfect excuse to continue to keep their vulnerability tucked away.

It's diplomatic to refer to Eights as assertive, but it's more honest to refer to them as aggressive, with all their energy spent pushing against the environment in a constant power struggle. This perpetual battle stance is exhausting, though, and while it might make Eights feel strong, it tires them out quickly because they're wasting that energy in every fight, rather than being discerning as they use their great stamina and protective instincts in the service of justice. Their big belligerence isn't sustainable over the long term, and they need to find another way to show up if they want to have the necessary moxie to keep leading with integrity and courage. Think, for a moment, Eights, of what kind of life-giving things you would have energy for if you just cut back on, like, half of all the hills you've been dying on lately.

You're not going to like this, Challengers, but you find freedom from your rowdy and reckless ways through the intentional cultivation of your **Virtue: innocence.** I know, the idea of trying to lean into something as vulnerable-sounding as innocence makes my skin crawl, too—I get it. But the visceral reaction you (and I) just had to the concept of innocence is the very reason this is your Virtue. It sounds so incredibly undefended and exposed that it's unsettling and feels antithetical to every force field you've erected between yourself and the cruel world.

And that's exactly what innocence is asking of you: to lay down your weapons and approach your perceived adversaries with your necks exposed. **Innocence invites Eights to trust your unguarded hearts to someone else, not to the reinforced walls you've built.** Innocence grants Eights the opportunity to be on the receiving end of the support that you give to others, to risk mutuality in your relationships, and to give yourself permission to seek shelter in others as much as you provide protection for those you love.

Well, my rowdy lil Protectors, when I had to reckon with the reality that it wasn't sustainable for me to keep showing up like a stone pillar—that in order to keep fighting the battles I really believed were worth fighting, I was going to have to learn to stop raging against every machine—I had something that resembled a crisis of identity. So, if that's what's happening for you, you're not alone. But Eights are good at denial (it's your Defense Mechanism, after all), so let me beat this dead horse just one last time in the hope of driving it home for ya.

Eights, I know you love to come across as tough and in control, but the truth is that your strength isn't in your might and muscle; it's in your ability to champion people in the realization and reclamation of *their* agency. And despite your best attempts to hide them behind layers of armor, your battle-scarred but resilient hearts are still soft with the capacity to extend forgiveness and mercy—the kind of gift this harsh world needs more of. I know you like to spend your enormous energy chasing storms for that thrilling rush of adrenaline that makes your pulse beat like a drum, but the electricity that already flows through your veins, without the need for revving your engines through adventure or adversity, is more than enough to help others make contact with their own vitality. Eights, by your vibrant spirit, you remind people that they, too, are alive, and by your gentle hearts, you remind people just how precious their lives are.

All right, ya crusty lil sweethearts, you survived the scandal of having your tender, sensitive, delicate hearts exposed to the whole world—by one of your own, no less! A betrayal of epic scale, if I've ever seen one. But I'm exposing you because I know (and I know that you know) that the source of your strength *is* your vulnerability, your tenderness, and the soft tissue of your redemptive hearts. I'm going to challenge you, darling Challengers, to start letting people in. It's in your surrender that you're at your strongest.

FROM BABY STEPS TO BADASS PATTERN BREAKING

All right, my always battle-ready Challenger, I know that taking concrete action is rarely an issue for you—in fact, your standard operating procedure usually involves making moves before giving them a second thought. But I also know (all too well) the visceral choking experience that comes along with allowing your vulnerability to be expressed and thus exposed. You've got to walk before you can run. So here's your first baby step: *Start* with observation and reflection, before going with your first gut instinct. Not only will you be giving yourself the time to gain more clarity, but you'll also already be breaking one of your patterns. Talk about a two-for-the-price-of-one deal!

Here are some reflection questions to help you observe and understand yourself with more clarity:

- That visceral choking experience I mentioned above? Pay attention to when that awful grip on your throat takes hold. That's your body's way of saying, *Hey, I'm feeling vulnerable, and I don't care for it.* What if you got curious about what feels like it's at risk when your body has such a strong reaction instead of rushing to armor yourself with decisiveness and domination? Every time you feel that somatic bristle, can you regard it as an invitation to be present to that sensation and let it welcome you into greater insight about your fears rather than rushing to launch a counteroffensive?

- Pay attention the next time you're with others and things aren't happening quickly enough for your liking. Maybe you're at work, and nobody seems willing to take the lead on a big project, or your friends can't decide where they want to go for dinner. You know that sense of impatience and urgency (and annoyance) that arises within you when nobody is stepping up to just make a decision? What if that's another opportunity for you to get curious about what's going on under the surface of your surliness? These emotions are sending up the signal that underneath your restlessness lurks some fear about a loss of control. What do you fear is at stake when you aren't in control. What do you fear is at stake when you aren't in person in your relationships prevent you from being able to be vulnerable in them? What do you think might happen if you don't come to a decision quickly?

BADASS PATTERN BREAKING

All right, ready to see what kind of intentional action all this reflection can make way for, ya eager lil Eight? (Of course you are.) Again, start small, and work your way up. **As you start to trust your** ability to surrender the driver's seat without losing your autonomy, take bigger and bigger risks. Here are some concrete suggestions:

- Let your friend pick the restaurant that you get takeout from or the movie that you fire up on Netflix. If you want to really stretch yourself, ask the server what menu item they like, and take their suggestion.
- Think about a regular task that's difficult for you, and ask a friend how they would approach it. Then do it their way. Want to really get out of your comfort zone? Ask your friend to help you with said task.
- The next time a big, important project is rolled out to your team at work or church or school, try resisting your instinct to raise your hand and volunteer to take it on. And hey, Eight? Don't just do that thing where you let someone else step up to be in charge but you still end up testing just how worthy they are of leadership. Relinquish your control entirely, and let someone else take the lead, without running them through your exhausting vetting process first. Give them the benefit of the doubt, and give *yourself* the chance to see that you're strong and capable enough to survive not being in control for once.
- The next time you notice yourself wanting to step in and make an executive decision for others when a plan isn't being reached quickly enough (by your standards, anyway), take a beat. See what happens when you allow a slower decision-making process to play out, without intervening and hurrying things along.
- Think about someone who you're *really* mad at. What if you set down the armor of your anger and got curious about what within you is hurting underneath your ire? Can you find the courage to express not just your anger but your hurt to them? And is it possible for you to give them an earnest and fair shot at redeeming themselves and earning back your trust?

TYPE NINE

Comfortably Numb (and Impressively Stubborn)

I'd warn you that this is going to hurt, Nines, but the truth is that, with the horse-appropriate dose of your own emotional narcotics that you're on, there's a good chance you won't feel anything at all as we go through this chapter.

This perpetually tired, numbed-out, asleep-at-the-wheel-of-their-lives archetype is probably *the* most well-loved of all the Types (sorry, Twos—I know you work hard for that title, but if it's any consolation, Type Twos are, at least, Type Twos' favorite Type). Despite being so well-loved by so many, Type Nines, unaware of their own importance, often abandon themselves for the sake of keeping the peace, living under the constant fear that the assertion of their own emotions, preferences, and opinions will rock the boat so badly as to toss them overboard and out of the safe harbor of their relationships.

By their own admission, Nines often resort to passive aggression and stealthy avoidance tactics, rather than plainly stating what they're thinking. This is the distinctly Type Nine brand. Nines assert control in their relationships in a way similar to how protestors go limp in the arms of the police dragging them off government property. They don't fight the transport, but they sure as shit don't help it either, becoming uncooperative dead weight to those attempting to address problems, resolve conflicts, or just figure out what Nines want to eat for dinner.

The archetypal name for Type Nines is the Mediator or the Peacemaker. Their grounded, sturdy presence brings a sense of calm into the environment. They have a gift for not only seeing all sides of an argument but also seeing the merit in each perspective—a gift that makes other people feel heard and valued in a way that no other Type can quite achieve. Receptive and non-judgmental, Nines are exactly the kind of people who can hold space for others without inserting their own agenda into the conversation. As their archetypal titles would suggest, they have a unique ability to reconcile perspectives across massive differences, bringing unity into fractured spaces.

That all sounds delightful, but that's not why I'm here, Nines. I'm here to wake you up to all the conflict your numbing out and self-dismissal causes. All your beautiful healing energy is the stuff that the rest of us dream of in our relationships and our world, but y'all can be a real nightmare too. At the core of my being, I believe that Type Nine is *the* most stubborn Type on the Enneagram. Just because you don't raise hell while you're digging your heels in doesn't make you any less stubborn (and frustrating) than the more combative Types.

The **Essential State** of Nines, at their most expanded, is the solid ground of unity and unconditional love. They possess an incredible innate understanding and ability to see that there is, and can be, a wholeness and unity to all of our world, where everyone belongs and everyone is valued. The fractures in our world and relationships that seem so irreparable can be

Peacemakers are receptive and spacious enough to see the value in complex and conflicting viewpoints without diminishing anyone.

transcended, as our Nines show us in their ability to equalize and embrace. Peacemakers are receptive and spacious enough to see the value in complex and conflicting viewpoints without diminishing anyone. When awake, Nines have a big, sexy, powerful, all-encompassing energy that is engaged and dynamic, peaceful and rock-steady secure. It repairs broken bonds and restores disconnections and misunderstandings to usher in new unions with a deeper appreciation for differences.

All of that sounds so lovely, and we can see why people love Nines. However, all of it is contingent on Nines actually being conscious and actively resisting their well-worn patterns of numbing out and spending their already dispersed energy with trivial distractions that don't actually matter to them. As we know by now, we live in a world that's still got to get it together, and the Nine ego structure develops in the context of this truly fractured, discordant world.

Somewhere along the line, Nines came to believe that the world is splintered enough, that peace and connection are tenuous and fragile, and that people are unimportant. The rest of us can certainly accept that there is truth in the Nines' perspective—**there is a lot of conflict, disconnection, and chaos in the world.** But being that it's their **Core Belief,** this fragmentation and chaos become the central features of the world as Nines observe it (ironic for a Type that can otherwise easily see all perspectives). Suddenly, relationships become minefields, connection hangs by a thread, and peace is a precariously placed glass vase on a flimsy, unreliable shelf. One wrong move, one careless comment, one hot take expressed, and all their relationships could come crashing down to shatter on the floor, leaving them alone and responsible for even more brokenness in an already-fragmented world. This Core Belief is what leads Nines to their pattern of disappearing from their own relationships at the first sign of tension, so convinced a conflict could destroy their connections that they never show up enough to be heard and taken seriously.

When the Nine's peace and connections feel like they're balanced on the blade of a knife, that superhuman ability to see the merit of all perspectives comes in handy—sort of. The **Focus of Attention** for the Nine, in their fragile and chaotic world, is **the opinions, priorities, and agendas of others,** effectively making other people, rather than themselves, their point of reference. The ability to see those perspectives is great, but the Nine, in an attempt to keep the peace and maintain connection in their own world and relationships, simultaneously assigns greater value to the perspectives of others and hooks themselves up to a steady drip of emotional narcotics as a way to dull their own opinions, priorities, and perspectives. This ability becomes a heavy weight, rendering them unable to distinguish themselves from the other. Without actually testing their hypothesis that closeness and union are brittle and unable to withstand the turbulence of our unstable world, the Peacemaker's Focus of Attention naturally lands on the convenient pieces of evidence that prop up their perspective (ironically, their evidence contains exactly as much structural integrity as they believe exists within their relationships).

The **Core Fear** of the Nine can be articulated in quite a few ways, but a lot of those articulations boil down to some version of this: **They'll be disconnected from the ones they love, thus confirming that they're just another unimportant, discarded scrap of material free floating in the fragmented world.** If they dare to assert themselves, their difference of opinion may end up being more important than the relationship (and, by extension, more important than they themselves are), and the people they love will give them the boot. The Mediator fears that they are only ever loved for the way they make other people feel and that any disruption to the peaceful atmosphere they work so hard to uphold will result in the breaking of relationships that they've prioritized over and above themselves. An underlying sense of inferiority plagues the Nine, planting the seed of their fear of their own lack of importance.

As I mentioned a bit earlier (much to the dismay of the Twos, ha), Nines are arguably the most well-liked Type on the Enneagram, and a lot of that good favor toward them comes down to

> *The Mediator fears that they are only ever loved for the way they make other people feel and that any disruption to the peaceful atmosphere they work so hard to uphold will result in the breaking of relationships that they've prioritized over and above themselves.*

how chill and laid-back they are. Go-with-the-flow and unassuming, Nines don't insert their agenda or stir up drama when they're bored (take note, Eights). Their **Idealized Self-Image** is that **nothing ruffles their feathers and they aren't in the business of escalating conflicts or tensions.** It's this Idealized Self-Image that, unlike their Essence, takes a nuclear reactor's worth of energy to maintain. It takes so much energy, in fact, that it leaves Nines depleted and unable to initiate much other than the maintenance of this self-forgetting façade. Not to jump ahead here, but this drain on their energy is exactly the thing that leads to the inertia that Nines are well known for, at their worst.

But before we go too far, let's keep parsing out the difference between the Idealized Self-Image and the actual Essential State of the Nine. We know that ego is a cheap rip-off of Essence, and we can see how these qualities of being laid-back, go-with-the-flow, and non-confrontational can certainly mimic peace, unity, and wholeness. But the Nine, being a Gut Center Type, has a whole lot of energy packed into their bodies, which comes with a pretty black-and-white sense of boundaries. They have a real rowdy internal defensiveness around their autonomy and sense of control and, of course, a close relationship with anger.

The Nine's Essence is expansive and receptive and, critically, is wide awake and engaged with its own strength. It takes up space and makes no apologies for that, comfortable with its naturally enormous presence. Alert and attentive to the immediate moment, the Essence of the Nine remains involved and active in their lives, exercising their agency by prioritizing their dreams and acting according to their interests, rather than deferring to everyone else's. Their Essence is expansive enough for everyone, including themselves.

The Idealized Self-Image places a perpetual drain on the Nine because of all the energy it takes for them to maintain their laid-back persona for the sake of others.

A far cry from that dating-profile-worthy description above, the Idealized Self-Image of the Nine, as the kids say, could never. Chill to the degree of *maybe we need to check them for a pulse,* the Nine in their Idealized Self-Image is conflict avoidant and disengaged, using all of that immense Gut Center strength to stubbornly stay fast asleep to their own preferences and prerogatives. In an attempt to maintain a relaxing atmosphere, the Nine appears noncommittal to the point of being unprincipled, allowing people to walk all over them because they've abandoned themselves long ago. But don't be fooled by what seems like the path of least resistance that they take. The Idealized Self-Image places a perpetual drain on the Nine because of all the energy it takes for them to maintain their laid-back persona for the sake of others.

If I had a nickel for every Nine that's ever commented how wild it is to them that they have the nickname "Peacemaker" when they've never really known peace themselves, I wouldn't need to take a paycheck again. Despite the placid waters on the surface, Nines will often talk about how disturbed and conflicted they feel internally. They have a finely calibrated barometer for tension and discord, and as soon as the internal pressure begins to rise, Nines retreat into their inner Zen garden, where they have control over themselves by virtue of stubbornly shutting it all down and becoming impossible to reach or move. It's not actual peace or tranquility but a numbness that feels safer than allowing anyone to see the intensity of Nines' own desires.

Let's take a beat here, Nines. I know this stuff is heavy and unpleasant, and if you haven't totally tuned out, then you're probably sitting in some serious discomfort—hey, good for you! I know it doesn't feel good, but actually engaging with this stuff enough to feel how gross it is, is an example of the kind of engagement that frees us from the muck of our patterns. Pausing here isn't just for the sake of feeling our feelings. It's important to remember that our Idealized Self-Image develops as a response to how we perceive the world—and we're not totally wrong in how we perceive the world! Per your Core Belief, dear Nines, the world *is* a fractured, tense, conflict-torn place, so going with the flow and helping maintain whatever shred of peace you can find in your day has helped you survive all the brokenness. Nines do earn love by keeping the peace and acting so incredibly easygoing. This Idealized Self-Image helped you navigate the turbulence of the world, and it did help maintain the connections you consider so precious. Not only that, but when people came to you to feel seen and heard, it also made you feel important. So as much as it will serve you more now to lower the mask of your Idealized Self-Image, it's important to extend compassion to it for the ways it got you to where you are today.

Every Type has a **Defense Mechanism** that holds together all their ego machinery and its shenanigans, and for the Nine, it's **narcotization, or, in layman's terms, numbing out.** The still waters of the Nine's Idealized Self-Image hide the raging-hot springs of fury and intensity underneath, and that's a lot to walk around with every day. In order to keep calm and carry on, the Nine has to employ a heavy dose of emotional narcotics on a strict schedule, keeping them asleep to the hot takes and inner rage-cage underneath as well as their sexy and spicy desires and, indeed, their own importance. This makes it easier to merge with the lives of others, thus ensuring close contact and connection (I mean—how much closer can you get to abandoning yourself than becoming the other?). More than just avoiding their anger at others, though, being so numb allows them to avoid facing the fact that much of their anger is with themselves, at their constant self-shrinking for the sake of other people's peace.

> *Being so numb allows them to avoid facing the fact that much of their anger is with themselves, at their constant self-shrinking for the sake of other people's peace.*

The swirling of sloth that Nines (and people in relationship with Nines) suffer is the result of a few pieces of their ego structure hard at work. When their Focus of Attention is on the perspectives, opinions, and prerogatives of others and they're motivated to maintain close contact and connection in a fractured world, all their energy is going to go to the prioritizing of those external concerns and the exhausting work of quieting their own internal rowdiness with busyness and distractions so that those external priorities have less competition. Is it any wonder that Nines are exhausted all the time? They spend their days trying to dilute the intensity of their own desires so that they can shoulder and support the desires of others, all in the interest of maintaining contact and closeness. Nines, what would it be like to risk encountering the full strength of your desires, without dulling them down? What do you think might have to change if you allow yourself to take your dreams as seriously as you take others'?

Of all the Vices, the Vice of the Nine seems to be the one that causes the most suffering in themselves and in the people who love them. That is, it causes frustration over what is seemingly the standard-issue laziness that comes along with that beloved laid-back persona. The people who love the Nine can't figure out how to motivate them to take initiative in their lives, and unfortunately, the Nine can't figure it out either. So, they remain stuck in a quicksand of their own apathy, passively observing their lives rather than living. **Inertia** is the predictable outcome of the conflict that perpetually churns within the Nine. They become torn between the terror of speaking up for themselves and their unbridled rage at being overlooked because they didn't speak up. Inertia allows them to instead remain at an impasse with themselves. Much like the immobility we get caught in when we've been sitting in the same place for so long that our legs go numb, **the inertia of the Nine keeps them stagnant.** Any attempt at moving forward results in pins-and-needles discomfort, prompting the inner-peace-starved Nine to numb back out.

Huge somatic anger is part of the birthright of the Gut Center, and despite what appears to be a fixed speed of slow motion, the Nine is no exception. The Mediator's Gut Center anger is reactive to the experience of being overlooked—often by themselves before anyone else—triggering their fears of being unimportant and disposable in their relationships. Covering themselves and their anger under a bulky blanket of blankness and feelings of inferiority, the Nine spends all that big, juicy strength on inessentials, leaving them with nothing for themselves. Their inertia is a half-hearted shrug in response to their inner rage at their perpetual indolence.

Outwardly appearing to be the least angry of the Gut Center Types, Nines coast through life like cool little cucumbers, just happy to be along for the ride. While the occasional passive-aggressive dig might belie their generally easygoing nature, they tend to avoid causing a scene or fussing, so most people find them to be quite agreeable and easy to please. But let your guard down at your own risk. Type Nines are a lot like a volcano. Years, even decades, can pass without incident, the rage dormant beneath a placid surface. Then suddenly, with very little warning, something finally tips the scales, and Nines wake up to the staggering amount of molten-hot fury that they've numbed themselves to, and all their unattended-to wrath comes showering down on their nearest and dearest.

The dormant periods of the Nine's anger are often long, and even when they're aware of their own anger, they usually deal with it by not dealing with it. They often avoid the person that they're angry with and sometimes go MIA from their relationships so as to not rock the boat and risk open conflict. The cruel irony of this withdrawal is that it often reinforces the Nine's belief that they're unimportant in their relationships, when their loved ones, unaware that their Nine is angry, upset, or hurt, don't pursue them to reconcile.

When the Nine does finally express their anger, it comes out sloppy and sideways, rarely focused on the actual issue that the long-suffering Nine has been stubbornly refusing to acknowledge. Forgetting to pick up the Nine's preferred peanut butter can make them feel overlooked and ignite their fuse. With the lid finally blown off, the flames of long-avoided anger leap out, and years of unaired grievances reduce what seemed to be calm relational landscapes to scorched earth. In all fairness to Nines, once you've been on the receiving end of their unhinged rage, it's not hard to understand why they're so committed to staying asleep to it.

In my work teaching the Enneagram, an observation I've found to be consistent across all nine Types is that, within the ego structure, conflicting forces give rise to an uncomfortable tension that the Type must navigate moment to moment. For the Nine, this tension is their desire for autonomy and agency and their equally strong and not-totally-incompatible-but-definitely-complicated desire for close, secure relationships that assure them of their importance. It's out of these desires that some of the worst of their bad behaviors are born: stubborn avoidance, relational absence, and lying.

Let's rip the Band-Aid off the worst of your offenses, dear Peacemaker. Yours is the particularly gnarly pattern of being a liar, liar, pajama pants on fire. Look, if it's any consolation, you're not the only liar on the Enneagram. Every Type has their own way

True and sustained connection requires honesty.

of distorting the truth for their own gain. But y'all can be habitual in misrepresenting the truth as a means to avoid conflict or disconnection in the relationships you cling to. Sometimes your lies are big stinkers, but more often than not, they're lies of omission—the result of feeling stuck under the self-imposed weight of maintaining peace and relational comfort. Lying doesn't actually keep the peace; it only delays the inevitable conflict. Buying yourself a moment of tranquility in the present with a little fib isn't worth the pain and damage to your relationships when the truth ultimately comes out. Peacemaker, true and sustained connection requires honesty, and momentarily disappointing someone who loves you with an honest answer will do far more to strengthen your bond with them than appeasement ever could.

Another common example of the Nine on their worst behavior is their habit of stealthy and stubborn withdrawing from their relationships in a bid to avoid conflict. If the tension between close relationships and self-determination is like a tug-of-war rope, the stubborn avoidance that the Nine defaults to is their best attempt to avoid choosing between the two warring sides of themselves. Sneaking away from their relationships without a word is more often than not the result of the Nine being aware of their own anger but absolutely unwilling to risk expressing it. Rather than speaking up for themselves, the Nine retreats and stays at a distance. They may ultimately return to the relationship after their anger has cooled and receded back under the threshold of their awareness. But it's just as likely that the rift may widen beyond repair as the fear that the Nine never mattered to begin with is confirmed by sustained silence (or insufficient efforts to win them back) by the other party.

The mental fixation of Nines is known as indolence, but it can be better understood as simply self-forgetting. Nines are considered other-referencing, making other people into their point of reference, rather than themselves. They often make decisions based on how their choices will affect others without even considering that they might have skin in the game too. By flying the white flag of surrender over their own dreams and yielding to the desires and priorities of others, Nines fail to show up in their relationships, interfering by way of their absence with the very connection they deeply desire. Perhaps I can offer a reframe to our tranquil and grounded Nines, the Type that sees the merit in different perspectives. I know you believe earnestly that you're sparing others from the same inner turbulence and conflict that plague you, but in abandoning yourself, the connections that you're working so hard to maintain aren't anchored in who you really are, because you aren't truly present to the relationship. Connections are much easier to let go of when they aren't secured by presence to begin with. So go ahead and show up in your relationships. Give people something solid to connect to in your true, full self.

The **Virtue** for the Nine is often referred to as **right action,** or

engagement. When held up in opposition to the inertia of the Nine, yeah, a little kick to the keister is clearly necessary here to counteract the inaction. Engagement is alert, awake, present, and, yes, engaging with the intensity within the environment and within themselves. Engagement for the Nine is **actively, fully participating in their lives, giving voice to their opinions, and taking the time to locate and honor their preferences and values by way of their decisions and actions.**

Engagement asks that the Nine use their strength to stay awake, not fall asleep to themselves and all their hopes for themselves. Right action invites the Peacemaker to show up and speak up, resisting the familiar comfort of other people, trusting that conflict can be constructive and conducive to increasing intimacy. Engagement demands that the Nine advocate for their own perspective just as much as they make space for the perspectives of others, taking control of their lives by being present, instead of defending their autonomy by closing off.

Okay, Nines, we've covered a lot of ground, and I can imagine that this has been tiring because you aren't great at figuring out how to spend all that big Gut Center energy in service of yourself. But since you're good at seeing the whole picture, let me offer you a vision of what you're capable of. If you can see value in differing perspectives, then my hope is that you can extend the same understanding to the different parts of yourself and your ego structure, holding them with compassion because they're just trying to help you survive in this chaotic and isolating world.

The gift of your Type is an expansive wholeness that has space and acceptance and love enough for everyone—not the least of whom is yourself. People already feel important and seen in the way that you engage with them; consider how much more treasured and meaningful you'll be able to make people feel when your engagement is anchored in secure trust in your own paramount importance. I know there is comfort and shelter in your numbness, but in the fragmented world that we live in, we need your all-

embracing awareness and all-inclusive receptivity to heal the disconnection between us and within us.

All right, Nines, you can open your eyes. This nightmare is finally coming to an end, and everyone now knows that there's a lot
more to you than your go-with-the-flow, unassuming façade. I
promise that if you show up, you're going to be pleasantly surprised
by how it feels to allow yourself to be seen and to receive the beautiful gift that you give everyone else.

FROM BABY STEPS TO BADASS PATTERN BREAKING

As we've covered pretty extensively by now, sweet Nine, a big
source of your suffering is how incredibly difficult it is for you to
take action. You're pressed down under the impossible and draining task of keeping the peace for everyone else, so of course it's
hard to drum up the strength to take up your own space. So much
of your energy goes toward making space for other people to be
seen and understood and valued. My hope is that these questions
can help you do the same for yourself so that you can get clarity on
your own desires and dreams and, ultimately, your own importance.

- Think about a person you've found yourself creating distance
  from or perhaps someone you've been totally avoiding like the
  plague. You're probably going to notice a distinctive
  disturbance in your comfort when you think about this person,
  and you'll have a strong instinct to numb out. Rather than
  anesthetizing or rushing to resolve it for yourself, let yourself
  investigate the emotional pins and needles that you're feeling.
  Is it possible that you're angry with or hurt by them? Do you
  feel overlooked by or unimportant to them? What do you
  think you're trying to protect within yourself by creating
  distance or avoiding them? What are you afraid would happen
  if you did express your feelings of anger or hurt to them?
  What would it take for you to trust them enough to tell them

you're angry with them? What would you need from this person in order to reconcile with them?

- Consider the last time you yielded to someone and agreed to something you didn't want to do. Maybe someone asked you to come to their kid's dance recital or a colleague asked you to cover a shift for them, and you said yes because you didn't want to upset them. What did the tension between their request and your desire to say no feel like in your body? When else have you experienced that sensation, and did agreeing to their ask bring you a sense of relief? What do you think you avoided by saying yes to them—or what were you afraid would happen if you said no to them? What do you think it's costing you to say yes to others instead of yourself? How does always being the go-with-the-flow person in your relationships prevent you from being truly seen and known in them?

BADASS PATTERN BREAKING

All right, it's time to take all this reflection into the real world and start taking up some real estate in your relationships, baby. Slow and steady is key, sweet Nine—don't burn yourself out by trying to do too much too soon. These patterns have served you until now, so go easy on yourself as you learn to break them. Here are some suggestions of how to start taking up space:

- Take a chance the next time there is a low-stakes decision to be made, say, which coffee shop to go to or what to make for dinner. Instead of letting others make the call, try proposing an alternative option and convincing people to accept it. You don't even really have to care that much, but I want you to give yourself the opportunity to see that not going along to get along doesn't always result in discord and disconnection.
- The next time you're presented with options and you're not sure about your decision, resist the urge to withdraw or just say

yes in the moment to avoid disappointing someone. Advocate for yourself. Say that you need a little time to think about it. Take up space by taking the time you need to get clarity on what you want. Just be sure you do actually follow up and make your decision known explicitly.

- Think about something you've been putting off. Maybe it's a simple chore or a new hobby you want to try, or maybe it's a distant dream of yours that you can't seem to find the energy or the will to pursue. Just start. Whether it's as trivial as folding the laundry so your space can feel less cluttered or as immense as signing up for a mixology class because you've always dreamed of opening your own bar, start somewhere. Your dreams are worth it. Something is better than nothing, and momentum can build when you make a small beginning.

- I know you're haunted by this fear that you're not as important to people as they are to you and that a conflict will destroy your connection, and withdrawing feels both comfortable and confirming of this suspicion. Instead, take the risk of staying engaged in the conflict as though you *are* important enough for your loved ones to duke it out with. Let others take you seriously because you bravely trust that your feelings matter enough to be known.

R *Is for* Reformer *(and* Resentment*)*

All right, Type Ones, I'm gonna challenge you to do your best to take to heart the feedback that will follow in these pages. I *almost* asked my editor to leave some grammatical mistakes in this chapter, just for you. Not to drive you nuts, but because I figured you'll need the little hits of superiority you get from correcting errors just to survive all the way to the end. I know having all your flaws discussed at length isn't your idea of a good time, but if you can sit through this and resist the urge to point out all *my* flaws, I promise you'll be better for it.

Often easily identifiable by their clenched jaws and barely concealed rage, Ones are the Goody Two-shoes of the Enneagram. This tight-laced Type is admirably unrelenting in their effort to leave the world a better place than they found it. Or failing that, they redirect their unrelenting effort into getting you to stop leaving your shoes all over the place, or stop loading the dishwasher so inefficiently, or stop chewing with your mouth open, or stop any of the other very human habits Ones are afraid reflect poorly on them.

Having high standards for themselves and the people connected to them is the way that Ones exercise their Gut Center grip on control. Ones, in contrast to the passive approach of Nines and the openly combative stance of Eights, gain control through correction and moral superiority, smugly taking their place at the lead because of their strict adherence to the rules and expectations of propriety.

Ones are often referred to by the archetypal title of the Perfectionist (although, in typical fashion, they'll jump in and correct you by saying that they prefer the title "the Reformer"). They can be both highly principled and faithfully reliable—and are actually a *lot* of fun when they can get out of their own way! At the same time, Ones can be rigid, unforgiving, and highly critical, and, well, there's no nice way to say this, so let's just call a spade a spade: They can be a real pain in the ass. Unable to let even the most insignificant of errors go without correction, when Ones get the tiniest taste of their own medicine (nitpicking and criticism), their indignation comes to a boil so suddenly that everyone in the general vicinity is at risk for incurring the third-degree burn of their self-righteous wrath.

In their efforts to maintain their reputation as a Good Person™, Ones commit themselves to the work of the improvement and refinement of everyone and everything in their immediate sphere of influence. Much like Eights and Nines, their fellow Gut Center Types, Ones have their own special brand of controlling, and it tends to take the shape of correcting what and who is wrong in their environment. They try to control the people and circumstances around them, and depending on the degree of failure they encounter, they'll turn the attempt to control inward. They strong-arm their own intense and messy emotions into their internal pressure cooker, hoping that the outcome will be rational and organized, rather than the blackened, bitter crust of resentment left by the heat of their clamped-down, unexpressed anger.

This embodiment of radical acceptance makes way for the absolute best of what Type One can be: living, breathing integrity.

The **Essential State** of Ones, how they arrived in this dumpster fire of a place we call the world, is **the grounded, serene state of acceptance of everything as already perfect.** This embodiment of radical acceptance makes way for the absolute best of what Type One can be: living, breathing integrity in action and an example of just how transformative it is when our decisions align with our professed values. Personifying integrity down to their very core, unpatterned and unbothered Ones are the unlikely and stubborn, if pragmatic, optimists of the Enneagram, lending their vision for the sake of improvement because they know in their bones that the world can be a better place. In an integrated space, Ones can provide the world with structure that is supportive without being rigid, and order that is creative without being restrictive. So why is that not what most of us think of when we think of Type One?

Oh, right . . . because most of us have experienced the insufferable, holier-than-thou version of Type One instead. The inflexible, uptight, exhausting, and exhausted perfectionist with a raging superiority complex that can't let *anything* slide. The thin air up there on the moral high ground that they've stubbornly clawed their way onto is their drug of choice. It gives them a hit of smug satisfaction for just long enough to offer a moment of relief from the incessant cruelty of their Inner Judge.

Type Ones value rationality and sensibility, and their **Core Belief** about the world really reflects this. **Ones see the world as a corrupted, unethical, rotten place**—and really, it's a hard Core Belief to argue with. The world is a foul place. It's egregiously unfair, it's messy, irrational, and uncaring, and there is a collection of trash more than twice the size of Texas floating out in the Pacific Ocean.* Somewhere along the line, something went very wrong.

Before the Ones get too excited that we all agree they're right, let me remind you that *all* the Core Beliefs of the nine Types have validity and truth to them. However, as is also true of all the Core Beliefs, the Core Belief of the Perfectionist is precisely calibrated to exclusively home in on the world's amoral eyesores, leaving them virtually unable to see any other perspective without intentionally looking for it. The mess, the unfairness, the imperfection,

---

*Doyle Rice, "World's Largest Collection of Ocean Garbage Is Twice the Size of Texas," *USA Today,* March 22, 2018, usatoday.com/story/tech/science/2018/03/22/great-pacific-garbage-patch-grows/446405002.

is all that Ones can see, regardless of where they look and regardless of what is actually in front of them. Their corruption-tinted lenses distort their vision so much that they can't look beyond the imperfections of the world, and they end up constantly reacting to the world as though it's only a place of unfairness and flaws.

With their Core Belief putting such a heavy-handed emphasis on all the havoc and defects in the world, the One's **Focus of Attention** serves as a heat-seeking missile for finding the concrete evidence that their Core Belief is correct. For the Reformer, their Focus of Attention lands on **anything that is wrong or needs correcting in their immediate environment, anything they can attempt to control and bring back into some semblance of order.** The One takes in the world in a very somatic way, and their attention is right here and right now, in the present, which means that their Focus of Attention on what needs correcting is going to be experienced as urgent and visceral. It needs to be corrected, and it needs to be corrected *right now*. Already caught in the weeds of their ego structure, the One then directs their attention and energy toward trying to correct whatever they can, lest any uncorrected flaws in their immediate sphere of influence become direct reflections of their own inherent corruption.

Reformers then assign themselves the roles of judge, jury, and executioner in the constant court case against their own mistakes and standard-issue humanity.

With Ones walking around in a world they believe is jacked up and rotten and with their attention constantly being pulled toward the mountain of evidence that confirms the existential pollution of our world, their **Core Fear** that emerges makes a lot of sense. It's a sinking fear that they themselves are also defective and bad at their very core. So bad, in fact, that, **despite their best efforts, despite their best intentions to make the world** around them a more fair, just, equitable place, that inner contamination will always outweigh the good they try to do. Reformers then assign themselves the roles of judge, jury, and executioner in the constant court case against their own mistakes and standard-issue humanity. When their Core Fear is triggered by something like someone pointing out one of their flaws, the switch flips on, and their self-defensive patterns spring into action.

This deeply rooted fear that something is rotten in the state of Denmark (and when I say "Denmark" here, I mean the very soul of the One) is what drives them to overcompensate with an **Idealized Self-Image** of being a **Perfectionist**™. Remember, the Idealized Self-Image is the cheap off-brand version of Essence. It's adjacent to the real deal, but because it's born as a protective measure and out of fear, it misses the mark. That's how I see the difference between alignment and perfectionism. **Perfectionism is rigid and unforgiving, constructed to conceal Type One's flaws and standard-issue humanity, which they fear reveal a core of corruption within them.** Alignment instead expresses trust and confidence in the One's ability to discern that which is right from moment to moment, giving them the freedom to make space within themselves for new, expanded understandings of goodness and truth.

Okay, that was a lot of fluffy language to explain the difference between two words that many would consider two sides of the same coin, but it's really important to understand the disconnect between the Essence and the Idealized Self-Image, because when we can spot the difference between the two, we can start to dismantle the cheap armor of personality that we've cobbled together as a means of survival.

Knowing what to look for, in terms of the distinction between being our best selves and being ghoulish, is great, but it's also important to understand *why* we're being ghoulish. Our Idealized Self-Image is part protection and part survival strategy, and it's effective as hell. We really do earn love and respect and validation for all the ways that we imitate our Essence. Ones *are* rewarded for being responsible, reliable, polite, disciplined, and anything else socially deemed "good." They're trusted with the care of important things, consulted for their logical and well-thought-out opinion, and relied on to provide structure and order when it counts. Highly competent and discerning (except as it relates to themselves), Ones often find themselves in leadership, whether formally or informally. They *do* earn love by being on their best behavior.

Not only that, but for Ones who are afraid that their flaws and mistakes are evidence of an internal brokenness beyond repair, being perceived as perfectionists who exceed most other people's standards can also really provide a very smug sense of satisfaction in themselves. Even if they aren't actually as perfect as everyone seems to think they are, at least they're better than most people.

Ones, I can feel the heat of your hatred through space and time now that I've exposed one of the grossest elements of your shadow side—your raging superiority complex. It's part of the defense system of your Idealized Self-Image, and we've all got some really ugly machinery parts in ours, so before the pulsing vein in your forehead explodes, let me at least appeal to your strong sense of fairness and assure you that I'll expose everyone else's worst as well.

Reaction formation supports the entire ego structure of the One by helping them find their sense of superiority in controlling their anger when they can't control their environment.

It's a bit paradoxical that the One can contain this inflated sense of superiority and this haunting suspicion of their own depravity, but these weird contradictions are held together by the **Defense Mechanism**, which, for the One, is good old-fashioned **reaction formation**. If you've ever taken a Psychology 101 class, you've probably encountered the concept of reaction formation. In brief, **it's when someone performs a reaction that is more socially acceptable than the genuine emotion they're experiencing.** Essentially, reaction formation supports the entire ego structure of the One by helping them find their sense of superiority in controlling their anger when they can't control their environment.

As an example, a Type One may laugh or cry, rather than expressing the white-hot rage that they're really experiencing. By smiling through gritted teeth so that their real emotional reaction remains behind their polite façade, the One is able to maintain their persona of perfection and superiority. All the while, the intensity of the emotions they aren't expressing continues to fuel their fear that their inner messiness is beyond remedy.

By smiling through gritted teeth so that their real emotional reaction remains behind their polite façade, the One is able to maintain their persona of perfection and superiority.

We've made some references to the anger of the One, but for a Type that is largely governed by it, we really haven't done it justice yet. The One's relationship to their anger is something of a dumpster fire for them. To understand their relationship with anger, it's helpful to remember that by virtue of being a Gut Center Type, they experience the world and their emotional reactions to it in an intense, visceral, and immediate way. So, for the One it's a bodily experience: It feels too intense for words and threatens to boil over and out of control. To contain so much of such an unpredictable and potentially destructive emotional force is terrifying to the One and further evidence of their inner corrosion. Forget about giving it space or expression—that molten lava can't be allowed to erupt.

Anger is both the dominant emotion that Ones experience *and* specifically their **Vice,** or the emotional experience of being stuck in their patterned prison. More so than Eights or Nines, Ones are dealing with a double dose of the stuff. It's the deeply satisfying fuel of their self-righteousness and, at the same time, a terrifying reminder of just how destructive they have the capacity to be if they allowed it to have full expression. Their Vice creates a cycle within them where **they're constantly plagued by an emotion that they feel like they're justified in experiencing yet have a responsibility to keep in check.**

With the One's Vice and the Gut Center's dominant emotion

both being anger, maybe we need to do a little unpacking of this theory that more anger is the One's response to their own anger. The anger of the Gut Center in general is focused on the breach of boundaries and loss of control or autonomy. The One, justifiably angered by their distorted belief that they can't make mistakes without compromising their credibility, gets even angrier. They have sort of set their own trap. Holding themselves to such an impossible and rigid standard and projecting it onto others tends to create the perfect climate for others to take gleeful delight in the humanity of the One when they do slip up. Regardless, anger begets anger in the One. Their ego structure responds with more self-righteous rage when they feel angry that their exhausting, self-imposed code of ethics grants them no wiggle room to be a human.

We've talked a lot about how the Perfectionist suffers at the hands of their own ego structure, but let's spare a mention for the way they make the rest of us suffer, shall we? I've touched on it a little bit as we've made our way through the ego structure of the One, but let's spend a little time really naming the impact of that pesky superiority complex that they tend to soothe and defend themselves with.

Common charges levied against Ones in the courtroom of their relationships include an excessive buildup of resentment and perpetual annoyance, constant attempts to control and correct their loved ones, and a brutal tendency to sentence themselves (and others) to punishment just short of the death penalty over small infractions and missteps. But all these offenses can be traced back to the Ones' efforts to perform perfection and defend themselves against the humiliation of accidentally revealing their humanity.

Resentment is a common experience for Ones, who are famous for assigning themselves the role of project manager, nitpicking and critiquing anyone attempting to assist, and then getting angry when they're left to carry the task over the finish line on their own. Ones fail to recognize that their attention to detail can be just as much a pain in the ass as it is an asset. People who were initially on board to help will abandon their efforts when they watch Reformers insist on dying on *every* hill, stalling out progress in their attempt to achieve perfection. Ones' bitterness is crystallized as the responsibility of not only finishing the work but also finishing it to impeccable standards is squarely on their shoulders. Ones, yes, you drive the rest of us bonkers with this behavior, but we know it's exhausting to you as well.

Another source of resentment for the One is their habit of putting off fun, play, and pleasure, usually indefinitely. In her book *Atlas of the Heart,* author and professor Brené Brown talks about resentment, specifically a shift that occurred in how she understood it. Brown writes that she always understood resentment as a function of anger but, in conversation with Marc Brackett, an emotions researcher and writer, it was pointed out to her that resentment is not so much a symptom of anger as a symptom of jealousy: "[Resentment is] an emotion that we often experience when we fail to set boundaries or ask for what we need."* Essentially, resentment grows when we see others enjoying what we've prohibited ourselves from accessing. This framing of resentment is really helpful in understanding why the One, rigidly bound by their obligations, seems so pissed off all the time. It's because they haven't given themselves the permission to play before all the chores have been completed, work has been finished, and expectations have been met. *Of course* they're bitter, resentful, and, yes, jealous when they see how much fun others are having, despite how messy and out-of-order the world remains.

If you're not a One, it's probably confounding as to why anyone would ever want to put off having fun or enjoying little pleasures in life, but remember that awful superiority complex that Ones sustain themselves on? That's the need that's getting met by neglecting their desire to enjoy a little levity. Their high horse grows

*Brené Brown, *Atlas of the Heart: Mapping Meaningful Connection and the Language of Human Experience* (New York: Random House, 2021), 33.

higher still when they can soothe their play-starved selves with the self-satisfied knowledge that at least they were doing something productive with their time, rather than indulging in childish shenanigans like fun.

I can feel the scathing heat of a thousand Type One eyes burning holes through the pages for that harsh take on their relationship with fun, but in the interest of self-awareness, I had to hit ya hard with that one, all right? That said, in the interest of self-compassion, let's really take stock of what's at work, now that the ugly reality is out there. The One's need for superiority is a symptom of their fear that they are not just inferior but irredeemably bankrupt at their core. The sense of superiority they get from their extreme discipline provides a temporary reprieve from their nagging suspicions about their wayward heart and its faulty ways. So, sweet Perfectionist, underneath your self-imposed embargo on fun is an earnest attempt to prove your goodness and soothe the anxiety around what your flaws reveal about your true character. This self-inflicted punishment only begets more frustration and resentment, fueling more fears about your inner flaws. Let me ask you, What kind of relief do you think might be available to you if you did let yourself enjoy a little fun without having to earn it?

Yet another of the principal ways that the Perfectionist gets on everyone's nerves is by being in everyone's business with their opinions, corrections, and exacting standards—disregarding the notion that there might be more than one way to get things done. There is this underlying (if not outright and obvious) sense of "I know better than you," and the One won't rest until you see that. This particular nonsense manifests itself in two ways. First, the One tends to use a maddening patronizing tone that they don't realize is insulting to the recipient. Second, when the One realizes that other people are perceiving them to be wrong, they launch a relentless campaign to prove their rightness, latching on to the issue and refusing to let it go like a Chihuahua sinking its teeth into the ankles of the poor soul just trying to feed it. Whether it's in the condescension with which they approach situations or the obnoxious lengths they'll go to in order to prove themselves right, their irrepressible need to be right is as exhausting as it is alienating.

Speaking of alienating, another standard feature in the ego of the One is an almost impressive ability to harbor a grudge—against others and against *themselves*. Rather infamous for their incapacity to forgive, the Perfectionist has trouble letting themselves off the hook for small mistakes and errors, which, of course, makes it challenging to let anyone else off the hook. The distorted thinking being that if the One isn't deserving of grace and understanding for their humanity, none of the rest of us unprincipled peasants are either.

So how does the One, so convinced of their irredeemability, free themselves from their prison of perfectionism? How do they unclench the vise that they call their jaw, unclench the other Vice they call anger, and find peace within this flawed, faulty world and their flawed, faulty selves? How do they give themselves permission to express all their anger, whether it's righteous or plain ole petty? This is where the **Virtue** of Type One can come in and illuminate the path away from pattern and back toward Essence.

In traditional Enneagram teaching, the Virtues are our expanded emotional capacity. An unpatterned and undefended Virtue manifests itself when a Type has allowed their heart to open. Whereas a patterned and pissed-off One is going to be angry, resentful, and unforgiving, an openhearted, expanded, relaxed One is going to spend their energy not correcting what is wrong but cultivating the Virtue of **serenity** by practicing patience and acceptance in each moment.

Serenity makes a radical request of the Perfectionist: to **accept that everything is *already* perfect and that their corrections and rigid self-discipline are unnecessary.** Serenity asks the Reformer to drop their armor of condescension and extend themselves the grace and space to be a work in progress rather than an example of perfection. Serenity invites the One into a much more relaxed stance, granting them permission to enjoy pleasure for the sake of pleasure, not as some long-awaited reward for their relentless attempts to purify the entire world.

Ones, the gift that you can offer in abundance and in freedom is an unshakable integrity and impeccable alignment with your values, an intuitive sense of the path toward a better, more equitable and wholesome world. You're multifaceted, complex, and, despite your best attempts to hide it, endearingly human. You're both gifted and burdened with a superhuman ability to notice the misalignments and inequities in our world, and by virtue of belonging to the Gut Center of Intelligence, you have the strength and energy to do something about all this mess.

Freedom from your unforgiving understanding of perfection, and the self-judgment that arises from awareness of your own flaws, is on the other side of coming to understand yourself and the world as an ever-unfolding project. Instead of the model of impossible infallibility that you are constantly trying to be, give yourself the permission, grace, and time to embrace the process of becoming.

Sweet, glorious, hot-mess-express, unavoidably human Type Ones, your integrity and stubborn optimism are true gifts to this world and to those who know you. And your sloppy, imperfect, flawed humanity could never take away from the ways in which you make us and our world a better place.

My hope for you is that you'll see that your imperfections and failings are all a part of the process by which you move more and more into alignment with the better world that you know can exist and that you'll be able to relax into that unfolding process, rather than beating yourself up. We need the best parts of you, which means that we need you to not punish yourself for your rough edges; hold them with compassion and patience, and give yourself grace, recognizing that your imperfections aren't symptoms of irredeemable rot within you but instead are warm invitations into your own beautiful evolution process.

Well, would you look at that? Someone else revealed your flaws and messiness, and you survived. Well done, Type Ones.

FROM BABY STEPS TO BADASS PATTERN BREAKING

As if you don't already have enough on your plate, dear Type One, I'm going to give you more. There's probably laundry to fold or a group project for you to do entirely on your own, but you and I both know that a significant source of your suffering is the exhausting whiplash between feeling terribly responsible to leave the world better than you found it and being completely overwhelmed. Not only does it seem impossible to make an improvement on this messy world, but you also feel alone in your efforts. Before I put more items on your to-do list, though, let's start with some reflection questions to help loosen the choke hold of those pesky patterns:

- We've focused a lot on resentment, so that strikes me as a good place to start with you, sweet Perfectionist. Resentment is acrid and isolating, and in a plot twist that we learned about from Brené Brown, it reveals to us what we're jealous of, rather than angry at. When are you most aware of your resentment? What do you think you might not be allowing yourself? What are you trying to demonstrate about yourself when you overextend yourself for the sake of doing it right? What do you think is at risk if something isn't done "correctly"? What do you think you're proving about yourself when perfection is the only acceptable outcome? What has it cost you? Can you see your resentment not as a bitter burden to bear but as an invitation to release your sense of responsibility toward *everything* and make more space to experience fun, playfulness, and acceptance?

- Speaking of releasing . . . let's spend some time reflecting on how hard you are on yourself. What do you worry might happen if you forgive yourself for a mistake or (gulp) a poor choice that you made? What has it been like to keep a running tab on every misstep you've made over the course of your life? How has that data set affected the way you see yourself? What would it be like to release all of it—yes, *all of it*—and give yourself the benefit of the doubt that you were doing the best you could at the time? What would it be like to trust that your mistakes can be redemptive, showing you how to do better next time?

BADASS PATTERN BREAKING

As promised, Reformer, it's time to turn self-interrogation into real-world implementation. The good news is that there is *no one* as determined as you to get it right, so be patient (and, yes, forgiving) with yourself as you learn how to embody an integrity that is shaped by your loving acceptance of yourself in all your magnificent humanity. Remember, capable, recovering Perfectionist, it's progress we're aiming for, not perfection. You've got this.

- Break a rule. Seriously. I'm not advocating that you break the *law,* Type One (that's more Type Eight's style anyway), but . . . find a low-stakes way to rebel against society's expectations of you. Show up late for a party or a work function. Give the barista a fake name. Wear mismatched socks. Serve red wine with fish to your dinner guests. Don't return your shopping cart to the corral when you're done loading your groceries into your car. Find a harmless way to let yourself be a little bad, and indulge in the thrill of it.
- Let someone you love help you out with a task, and resist the urge to correct their work and bring it up to your standards. Big oof, right? I know. But this is a way that you can kill two

birds with one stone. Not only will you be taking something off your already-overloaded plate, but you'll also be yielding to someone else and accepting their standards as *enough*, which is all that those of us who love Type Ones want you to do.

- Make time each week for something fun and lighthearted. Protect that time ruthlessly, and don't give it away to the demands of your to-do list. There will always be things that need to get done, and it's not the lack of getting things done that is making you irritable and frustrated; it's the lack of pleasure and play. Make play a critical priority, and show the world just how much of a hoot and a half you can be.

- Forgive yourself. I know you knew it was coming, but that doesn't change how important it is for you to extend clemency to yourself. That heavy load of self-blame you've been carrying? Set it down, and go forward, moving closer and closer to your best self with every unencumbered step you take.

Part III

THE HEART CENTER

INTRODUCTION TO THE HEART CENTER

Types Two, Three, and Four make up the sugary-sweet, relational, and emotionally led triad known as the Heart Center of Intelligence. A trio of sweethearts and superstars, the Heart Center Types share relational warmth and hearts that are drawn toward others. Twos are known for their generosity, sweetness, and martyr complex. Threes have an ease at relating to others, an impressive résumé of accomplishments, and a somewhat-unsettling ability to shape-shift into the version of themselves that is most appealing to whatever audience they're in front of in any given moment. (It should be noted that this shape-shifting isn't unique to the Threes. Twos and Fours are just as capable of the same self-curation, and you'd better believe we're gonna talk about it.) Fours, the tormented artists of the Enneagram, can be endlessly and delightfully creative, intoxicatingly romantic, and even moodier than a teenager experiencing their first heartbreak—unfortunately, unlike a moody teenager, it's not just a phase for the sullen Fours.

The Heart Center of Intelligence is distinguished from the other Centers by Types that mediate their meaning and identity in the world through their emotional experience of it. It's almost as though their hearts are magnets, pulled toward others. For Twos, the true north that their heart needle points to is the unmet needs of others. Threes gravitate toward the actions that will bring value to the world. And Fours are compelled by depth, beauty, and significance in people and the environment around them. Heart Center Types are those that can demonstrate both the beauty and the suffering of prioritizing connection. They can also be a manipulative bunch of snakes, charming and disarming their way through life, rarely directly asking for what they need, and often making it everyone else's problem when they don't get what they want.

Here are some things that come naturally to Heart Center Types:

- an ability to attune themselves to others and the world outside themselves
- an innate appreciation for nostalgia and the past
- an emotional landscape that has depth and range (if they choose to recognize it)
- a desire to make their relationships into mirrors of their identity and worth
- an ever-present current of shame that haunts them as they search for evidence outside themselves that they're worthy of love

Heart Center Types are a sentimental bunch, often longing for something that no longer exists (or maybe never did exist in the first place). This gift invites us all to remember that which moves us and matters to us. It calls up a wistfulness that reminds us of the power of our hearts—that is, the capacity to move beyond our basic self-preservation survival instinct and into deep connection with others. The trouble with this melodramatic orientation is that we can get stuck, relitigating a past that is long gone. The pipeline between nostalgia and self-involved navel-gazing is a short one, and dwelling in the past for too long keeps us from being present to what is available to us right now.

This dreamy longing looks different in the three Heart Center Types. Twos long for the early days of their relationships, when everything felt fresh and seductive and they hadn't yet neglected their needs to the point where resentment toward the other became unavoidable. Threes long for the time before they proved how impressive they could be, before the world awaited their next victory with bated breath, when they were free from the pressure imposed on them by all they've accomplished. Fours wander through their lives with a vague but intense feeling that they're missing something, so they long for the time before that loss took place, even if they're not quite sure what that loss was. Fours also often romanticize past relationships and set themselves up to pine for those.

Attunement is the superpower of the Heart Center Types, and it's also the source of much of their suffering. When they're in a healthy, undefended space, Twos' attunement takes the form of a spidey-sense for the unmet needs of others. Twos can intuit what others are missing and support them in fulfilling themselves. When on their patterned feedback loop, though, Twos project their own unmet needs onto others, aggressively giving to get and inflating their own sense of superiority by becoming indispensable in their relationships.

Threes attune themselves to what is valuable, improving the world around them by achieving what is needed. That attunement gets glitchy when Threes confuse their capacity to achieve with their innate worth. When this distortion takes over, Threes become competitive and ruthlessly results driven, with the ends justifying whatever disingenuous means they employ to get what they want.

Fours attune themselves to depth, meaning, and beauty in the world around them, possessing a unique perspective that invites other people into deeper reflection and meaning-making in their own lives. But that's not how most of us think of the Fours in our lives, right? Right. Because most of us tend to think of (and, in fairness, experience) Fours as melodramatic, perpetually dissatisfied with their present circumstances—regardless of how badly they wanted what they now have. They're volatile in their affections, sometimes utterly in love with us and other times utterly repulsed by us (often traversing this spectrum several times over the course of one conversation).

While it's often only the Fours who get the credit for it, all the Heart Center Types can have a remarkably vast emotional landscape. Twos, when healthy and evolved, can experience a depth of love for themselves and others, celebrating others without seducing them into providing for their neglected needs. In my opinion, Twos don't get enough credit for how skilled they are at avoiding negative emotions in their relationships. They haaaaaate acknowledging that they might have frustration, anger, or bitterness toward someone they love—because acknowledging those feelings would disrupt the image of themselves as *the* ultimate source of love, which helps inflate all that pride they get high on. Threes often get the reputation for having as much depth as a kiddie pool, much more concerned with their image than the substance of their souls. But Threes can and do possess depth; they just prefer not to have to reckon with it, in case it's not popular with their audience. Fours have a reputation for being deep and comfortable with expressions of emotion, and if the situation is boring or ordinary, they aren't above ramping up the expressions of emotion just to make things meaningful.

Heart Center Types, perhaps predictably, place particular and special value on their relationships. This can be a beautiful feature of this triad, teaching the rest of us how to honor other people and the bonds we share with them. That said, the Heart Center brand of relationality isn't always so selflessly motivated. Twos, Threes, and Fours have a tendency to use their relationships as mirrors, searching for the reflection of their value in the faces of others. Twos create conditions of dependency in their relationships, looking to others to assure them that they're deserving of love as a result of their helpfulness and generosity. Threes look to their relationships for a sense of identity; who they are is voted on by the studio audience. Fours look to their relationships to be mirrors of their significance. They want others to appreciate how special they are so they can be assured that their existence does actually matter in the grand scheme of things.

The common emotional suffering of the Heart Center Types is that of shame, the likely result of their tendency to base their identity on what is pleasing, valuable, or special to others and not themselves. Twos feel shame because of their needs. Their needs thwart their attempt to be a perfect martyr for the other. Threes feel shame as it relates to the less impressive parts of themselves. Anything that doesn't dazzle might tarnish their carefully cultivated façade, revealing the inner emptiness that haunts them. Fours feel shame over the discrepancy they perceive between what everyone else seems to have and their seeming inability to attain it. That deficiency feels like something special and important about them is missing, and it fuels the performance of their own uniqueness that they put on for everyone they encounter. This Heart Center shame inevitably leads all three Types to shape-shift into some uncanny, slightly off version of themselves—carefully curated to appeal to the person who can make them feel valuable and important—but they're always aware that the costume doesn't quite fit right.

Twos, Threes, and Fours are the Care Bears of the Enneagram; their superpower is hearts that beat in tandem with the hearts of others. Haunted by shame and a fear that causes them to question whether they deserve love, the Heart Center Types head down the path of perfunctory performance and productivity for the sake of praise. They switch between masks as gracefully as an acrobat leaps between trapeze bars, but they struggle to land on the solid ground of their own sense of self. At their best, however, Twos, Threes, and Fours can invite all of us into deeper relationship, not only with one another but also with ourselves as we connect with the incredible and vast range that our hearts are capable of experiencing.

TYPE TWO

Self-Sacrifice with Some Serious Strings Attached

All right, my sweet Type Twos, I'm going to warn you to brace yourselves for what's up ahead in this chapter. This isn't going to be pleasant. It's my observation that, of all the nine Types, Twos tend to be afforded the most grace and benefit of the doubt for their flaws. After all, you're just trying to be helpful! You just want to make our lives easier! You just want us to know that you love us! We can't fault you for that, right?

Well . . . yes, we can actually, and that's just what we're here to do. Your selfless reputation is admirable, Twos—it truly is. But it's *also* an incredibly convenient way to deflect accountability for the manner in which your helpful intentions can (and often do) result in harmful impacts. If I had to guess, I think folks in the Enneagram world tend to go easier on Twos than on most other Types because the lengths that even average Twos go to take care of others are often so incredibly drastic that it's hard to *not* see the toll that takes on the Twos. They have this way of eliciting empathy from us because we know they have to be suffering under the weight of everything that they're carrying for everyone else.

Not only that, but I also think something about Twos is very easy to identify with. Almost all of us, at some point, have been on the short end of a lopsided relationship, in which we're giving so much more than we get in return. That lack of mutuality is a constant for Twos (yes, often by their own design—we'll get into that later), and we can all remember experiencing that particular loneliness. So . . . we let any frustration we feel with them slide. They're already suffering enough; they don't need criticism from us, the people they're trying to take care of.

The truth of the matter is, though, by withholding honest feedback about the real consequences of our beloved Twos' overextension on our behalf, we're also withholding valuable opportunities for Twos to realize that we love them for who they are, not just what they're able to take care of for us. Being honest with them about how their constant self-sacrifice is harmful to them *and* to us is the only way we can help them liberate themselves from these painful patterns. Wow, that's a great way to reframe how I'm about to drag the Twos through the mud. Talk about putting lipstick on a pig!

We're all already familiar with some of the greatest hits of the Type Two descriptors: sweet, giving, loving, affectionate, generous, selfless, and warm. These darlings of the Enneagram are well liked and deeply appreciated, although they're quick to swat away a compliment or expression of gratitude. But as much as they may perform humility, they know exactly how indispensable they are, because the dynamic of dependency in their relationships is by their own careful engineering. Offers to reciprocate the Two's generosity are often declined, but you'd best believe that the Two is paying attention to who took them at their word instead of reading their mind.

All the Heart Center Types are contortion artists in their own right, twisting themselves into their most palatable form, which will earn them external praise and validation, temporarily soothing their fears about whether or not who they are at their core is worthy of love. For Twos, selflessness is the shape they shift into, prioritizing everyone else above themselves and their own basic needs, finding evidence of their worthiness in how much they're willing to sacrifice to take care of others.

In most Enneagram literature, Twos are referred to by archetypal names like the Giver, the Nurturer, the Caregiver, and the

Helper. All of these names communicate the principal feature of Twos: how much they do for others. If you ask a Two why they spend so much of their time and energy taking care of other people, their earnest answer is often something to the tune of "I just want people to feel loved." I believe Twos believe that sentiment of themselves with their whole hearts.

Twos are remarkable in their ability to meet the very universal human need to feel loved—in others and in themselves.

The **Essential State** of the Two is a space of **freedom that is rooted in a grounded and honest knowledge of who they are.** This stable footing allows the Two to truly make people feel loved without condition, by recognizing and meeting their needs without expecting anything in return. When sincerely embracing their Essential State, Twos are remarkable in their ability to meet the very universal human need to feel loved—in others and in themselves. It's a beautiful capacity, and it's one that the world needs more of.

Alas, a lot of Twos out there aren't really engaged in embracing their Essential State. Much happier to bask in the warmth of the positive adjectives assigned to them, Twos can get stuck on insisting that they be known by their intent, rather than taking accountability for their actions. And with a Type description that reads like the glowing obituary of a beloved celebrity, who could blame them? Generous, sweet, nurturing, selfless, relational, kind, thoughtful; Twos can almost be forgiven for stubbornly refusing to interrogate and get beyond the surface of their self-sacrificing mask . . . almost.

But as brightly as their beautiful qualities shine, the shadow of the Two is dark and cold. Manipulative, conditional with their love, and deeply entitled, they give to get. When their needs have been neglected for long enough, they can become venomous and vengeful, because by simply enjoying the kindness of the Two, the recipients of their generosity aren't holding up their end of the bargain (they never knew they agreed to).

The toxic pattern of the Two is two-pronged: self-sacrifice and self-neglect. They overextend themselves right into the lives of others, taking responsibility for fulfilling the needs of other people while willfully turning a blind eye to their own neediness, lying to themselves and everyone else that they somehow need less than the rest of us. They create a culture of dependency in their relationships and silently keep meticulous records of how much they've done for others so that when they can no longer ignore their own needs, they have money in the bank and the expectation that others will do as much for them.

This pattern develops and is then sustained by the **Core Belief** that the Two holds as a fundamental truth: There is only a finite amount of love in the world, and in order to have any legitimate claim to it, **love must be earned.** Again, we're faced with the pesky truth that the Two is right. There is a global shortage of love, a fresh shipment is on permanent back order, and we're living in a capitalist hellscape where even love and affection are commodities and not simply our birthright by virtue of our humanity. The world can feel like a cold, uncaring place to so many people, and that's before we take inventory of all the horrible things that we seem resigned to tolerate despite absolutely having the agency to make necessary changes to address them. So, when the Two looks around and sees how cruel the world seems to be, it's easy for the rest of us to understand how they reached the conclusion that there just isn't enough love in the world for all the people contained within it.

In a world that, according to their Core Belief, is sparse on love, the Giver's **Focus of Attention** is going to fall to the places where they can most easily find that lack of love, the most obvious being **unmet needs.** So, the Two's gaze fixes on the necessities that other people are going without, and they intuit where they can intervene in this compassion shortage and fill in the gap with

This Focus of Attention also allows the Two to attend to other people's needs as a convenient way to avoid acknowledging their own.

their own warmth and kindness. This Focus of Attention also allows the Two to attend to other people's needs as a convenient way to avoid acknowledging their own. As they preoccupy themselves with other people's needs, they silently start to wonder whether someone is looking out for *their* unmet needs, the places in *their* lives that don't feel very loved.

Twos overextend themselves and willfully disregard their own desires.

The **Core Fear** that extends from this belief is that **they must work extra hard to earn any love they hope to experience.** And from an early age, Twos *do* learn that they can earn love by being helpful and anticipating the needs of those around them. Fearing that they're deserving of love only inasmuch as they're being recognized for how giving and generous they are, Twos overextend themselves and willfully disregard their own desires. Their performance of selflessness earns them the affection of people around them and the assurance that they're lovable.

This strategy of avoiding their fear is built into their **Idealized Self-Image** of being **intuitively generous, tireless in their ability to give, and a constant source of praise and affirmation for people around them.** While we all put a lot of time and energy into defending and performing our Idealized Self-Image, Twos might take the cake for being most attached to theirs. They absolutely *love* to be seen as generous, selfless sweethearts. Good lord, do they love to be known as people who give, give, give and *never* take. They wear that martyr complex with pride and insist that it covers the multitude of sins they commit when they give their pattern of self-neglect and self-sacrifice full rein.

As far as Idealized Self-Images go, "giving, generous, and selfless" doesn't sound so bad, but make no mistake—it's just as insidious as the more obviously harmful masks that other Types use. Let's take the time to note the differences between the gorgeous, unconditional state of the Essential Two and the performative hubris of the contracted, patterned Idealized Self-Image. At their most expansive, Twos love freely, under no contract, and with no strings attached. There is no performance, no bid for assurances, just bighearted and abundant love, enough for everyone.

The Idealized Self-Image, by contrast, has as many strings attached as the inside of a piano, tense with the expectation that someone will reward them for their willful self-negligence and their intrusive brand of generosity. Unlike the Essential State, which gives without needing to receive credit for its giving, the Idealized Self-Image keeps track of all the unreturned favors and unpraised acts of service that it has shoehorned its way into providing for others.

Now, listen, whenever I'm presenting a workshop about the Enneagram, this is the point in the lecture that I take a pause to issue a critically important reminder to our mortified Twos. I know it can be brutal to have the impact of your intrusive and transactional ego assessed separately from your best intentions, but it's important to remember that these patterns didn't develop and sustain themselves in a vacuum. You *have* earned love by being self-sacrificing, giving, and intuitively caring. People have relied on you to take care of them, and your need to be seen and appreciated has been met by your willingness to go the extra mile to make someone feel loved. Without a doubt, the strategy of your Idealized Self-Image has been successful and has helped you survive in a world that is starving for love. So, while it's time to free yourself from the strings of giving to get, remember that this mask was as much a lifeline as it was an unhelpful pattern. Give yourself some grace for just trying to make it through the cold world with the best tools you had at the time.

That compassionate detour aside, let's get back into the gnarly stuff. It's time to chat about the **Defense Mechanism** of the Twos, which keeps the whole pattern locked into place. In their effort to sustain the completely

Twos have a tendency to confuse their aggressive repression and stubborn self-negligence for selflessness and generosity.

unnecessary practice of setting themselves on fire in order to keep others warm, Twos resort to **repression of their needs and of anything yucky within themselves that might threaten their image as selfless saints.** One of the more challenging aspects of their Defense Mechanism is that Twos have a tendency to confuse their aggressive repression and stubborn self-negligence for selflessness and generosity, making it very hard to extract themselves from the trap of their own setting. While appropriate in psychological terms, the word *repression* doesn't quite capture the no-holds-barred, fight-to-the-death cage match between Twos and their needs and emotions.

The Defense Mechanism, in general, is a great way to distinguish between different Types, and because I think Twos are one of the more mistyped of Types, this is a good place to do a little demonstration. People often find themselves stuck between Two and Nine. Twos and Nines are Types that tend to make other people into their point of reference, with Twos zeroing in on the needs of others and Nines focusing on the perspectives and opinions of others. That can look very similar, though (some people are very opinionated about their needs, after all), so here is where the Defense Mechanism helps us parse out the subtle differences. Nines' Defense Mechanism is narcotization or numbing out. This is decidedly *not* the case with Twos. With repression being an all-out brawl between Twos and their needs and the selfish emotions they hate to acknowledge, they're aware of their needs and feelings—they just really, *really* hate them.

Repression keeps the Twos' ego structure in place in some very useful ways. First and foremost, by repressing all their needs, Twos can remain focused on other people's needs and keep depositing into their bank account the currency that they believe earns them a share of the limited-edition product that is love. Second, by neglecting their own desires, Twos believe that they're never burdening others with their gross human needs, and thus, they never withdraw from that bank account. All of this lets them keep that selfless, sweet Idealized Self-Image perfectly in place, charming the pants off everyone they swoop in to nurture.

Now, we can't talk about Twos without talking about that nasty little **Vice** that is both their suffering and their sense of superiority: **pride.** Twos are proud of a lot of things, but two things in particular top the list. First, how

Twos' pride is, quite simply, their inflated sense of self-importance filled with the hot air of their martyr complex.

much they do for others, and second, how little they ask for (or even allow themselves to receive) in their relationships. Their ego is buoyed by both the empty calories of the external praise they earn for taking care of others and the stamina that allows them to keep going without receiving support from others. Twos' pride is, quite simply, their inflated sense of self-importance filled with the hot air of their martyr complex.

Pride is the fuel for the righteous rage that consumes Twos when people have the audacity to *actually* take them at their word when they insist that they don't need anything, *rather* than reading their minds and anticipating their needs just like Twos do for everyone else. Don't their loved ones know how quickly this would all fall apart if Twos stopped taking care of everyone? Don't they realize how much the Givers have given to them?

Underneath this parasitic relationship between their growing resentment and the pride that feeds it is the shame that is constantly raising the questions that plague Twos (and Threes and Fours): "Who am I?" and "Is who I am deserving of love?" They're heavy questions to constantly be searching for the answers to, and as a measure of overcorrection, the ego structure of Twos responds to that shame with the prickly bristle of self-importance.

I can imagine you haven't really been thrilled about this line of conversation thus far, Twos, but I've got to warn you, it's about to get much, *much* worse. Remember how I said you have a strong preference for insisting that your good intentions are given far more consideration and weight than any unfortunate but unintentional impact? Well, you're shit outta luck today, because we're about to do the opposite. We're gonna take a real, unflinching inventory of all the harmful impacts of your poor boundaries, inflated sense of self-importance, and conditional, quid-pro-quo brand of lavishness. Your self-neglect, oversensitivity to rejection, and martyr complex hurt people, and you need to face the consequences of that without hiding behind the shield of your good intentions.

Let's start by talking about what's probably your worst offense: the way you use niceness and generosity in your cloaked project of subtle manipulation. Twos are rather notorious for the seamless and covert way they end up in control in their relationships. Their mental fixation is flattery, and boy oh boy, do those sweet-talkin' Twos know how to make people feel special. Twos wield flattery with military-weapons-grade precision, winning people over by heaping praise and wide-eyed wonder on them. Unconsciously, Twos are attempting to instruct others how they themselves want to be dealt with. Flattery endears Twos to others and gives them express-lane access into the inner circle of anyone on the receiving end. Flattery is their doorway into relationship, where they can then tip the scales of relational power in their direction by showering people with over-the-top gestures of generosity and displaying the superhuman ability to anticipate the needs of others while never burdening them with their own pesky needs. In reality, Twos are quietly waiting until it dawns on their loved ones how much they need them and how indebted they are to them, and at long last, all their needs will be cared for by their newly aware loved ones, overwhelmed by gratitude for the Twos' long-suffering.

Except that it's rare that the person on the receiving end of all the Two's validation and love realizes that an invisible tab has been running this whole time and that the Two is expectantly waiting to be paid what they believe they're owed. With their Defense Mechanism of repression perpetually humming along in the background, the Giver earnestly insists that they don't need anything from the person they're in relationship with—they're just happy to be there.

As the bill of unrequited favors grows longer and longer and the object of the Two's charity continues to take them at their word that they don't need anything, Twos become increasingly desperate to be seen as the ultimate source of love and support in this person's life. Hence, the gestures of generosity get more and more pronounced. Greater sacrifices are made for the sake of the other, requiring the Two to go to even greater lengths of self-neglect. Surely, as the acts of service performed by the Giver become more and more grandiose, their beloved will take note and be struck, like Saul on the road to Damascus, with overwhelming gratitude and the urge to nurture their Nurturer.

That might happen . . . except that *still,* high on their own supply of pride-fueled self-importance, the Two refuses to express their own needs in their relationships. They refuse to acknowledge sadness over the fact that their relationships have become one-way streets, by their own hand. They refuse to give witness to their anger at the ways in which they chose to sacrifice themselves for the sake of their relationships, which they believe are reflections of their worthiness of love.

So what is actually going on underneath this weird tension between how the Two regards the needs of others with such urgency and sensitivity and how they regard their own with such contempt and abandonment? The ugly truth behind this conflict is that by keeping others indebted to them, the Two always has the upper hand in their relationships and, crucially, in the court of public opinion. Even if they're rejected, which is unpleasant for all of us but particularly devastating to the Two, being the loving, selfless one gives them plausible deniability of their own participation in the deterioration of the relationship. Friends rally around the sweet, heartbroken Two, who, by all appearances, was nothing but supportive and selfless to their partner, asking for so little in return for their kindness and devotion. They'll never admit it, but a scorned Two loves to wage a smear campaign, tearfully recounting how much they've tolerated in their attempts to heal their now-ex with their love. Even in the public-relations war they wage, though, the Two is cautious not to tip their hand and give voice to any hostility or anger toward the person who hurt them. Still trying to sell the image of being capable of the most pure, altruistic love the world has ever known, the Two might only offer some pitiful desire that their paramour could see themselves like the Two sees them (cue eye rolls from everyone listening).

That was an ugly pattern to uncover and lay out for everyone to see, but, Twos, it had to be done. As the old saying goes, the truth will set you free, but first it'll piss you off. Now that you're good and pissed off, what do you think has been the cost of the covert power games that you play in your relationships? And can you really keep bearing the heavy burden of all that power over your relationships?

Now seems as good a time as any to talk about the fairly anemic range of emotions that Twos actually allow themselves to experience. While Twos are often thought of as one of the more emotional Types on the Enneagram, the truth is that they have a fairly narrow repertoire of emotions that they accept within themselves and a pretty extensive list of emotions that they really hate to believe themselves capable of feeling toward a relationship or another person.

Twos express sweet, tender emotions with reckless abandon, but suspiciously absent from their grandiose expressions of their emotions are what I like to call "the spicy feelings." Feelings like anger, resentment, annoyance, and plain ole dislike. These spicier emotions and opinions about other people get repressed right alongside the Twos' needs, wrestled down lest they detract from the angelic, sweet, ultimate-source-of-love role that Twos perform in the world. These more heated sentiments have a tendency to reveal the places where Twos are feeling dissatisfied with their relationships, and if they acknowledge those feelings, then they're going to have to do something about them. Like, ask for more from their partner or friend or boss, which would totally upend the finely calibrated, subtle power dynamics they've worked tirelessly to build into the relationship. Can't be having that now, can we?

All of these obnoxious routines of conditional martyrdom and sneaky superiority can be mitigated by the cultivation of their **Virtue: humility.** In contrast to the beastly Vice of pride that pumps their ego full of entitlement, arrogance, and delusion around their needlessness, **humility helps bring a Two's swelling sense of self back into proportion, allowing them to return to a grounded stance in their relationships and roles.**

Not too long ago, my spiritual director and I were having a conversation about humility in my own life (hey, we all need it, not just the Twos), and she offered me a definition of humility that I think can be incredibly supportive to Givers. She said that *humility is being both no more and no less than exactly who we are.* It's especially challenging for Twos to be no *more* than exactly who they are, but I think being no *less* than exactly who they are presents its own set of obstacles to a Type that wants to be seen as having absolutely no needs at all. But I truly believe this understanding of humility can help deflate the pride caused by the dependency the Two has cultivated in their relationships.

Being no more than exactly who they are presents a direct challenge to Givers' prideful impulse to hyperbolize their place in their relationships. In that vein, humility asks Twos to get honest with themselves about how much the people in their lives are capable of—if the Twos would only get out of their way and allow them the chance to prove it.

On the other side of the same coin, being no less than exactly who they are confronts Twos with another direct challenge: how little they burden their loved ones with their own needs. In asking Twos to be no less than exactly who they are, humility demands that they show up in their relationships in a real way, as human beings who are allowed to need (and receive) support and care from their friends and partners, instead of the saintly martyrs they attempt to portray themselves as.

I warned you this was going to be unpleasant, Twos, but you survived! I knew you could do it. The gorgeous, love-worthy gift you offer the world is your ability to reflect to us the way that we deserve to be loved and to have our needs met completely, abundantly, and without condition. It's a remarkable gift that helps us feel held and supported in a world that can be cold and lonely, and that *is* something you Twos should feel proud of. But for all the love you put out into the world, the liberation that comes with humility is possible only when you open yourselves up to receiving just as much as you give. As the old saying goes, *the only way over is through.* You must meet your shame and pride and all your self-importance with this humble realization: You are no more important and obligated—and no less deserving of love—because of the loving, supportive, and tenderhearted friend, partner, colleague, and person you are.

It's been said that when a Two finally wakes up to their patterns, they experience a particularly intense devastation that can feel all consuming, threatening them with a bitter answer to that perpetual question about whether they're worthy of love. But by remaining present to the desolation that comes with an honest accounting of the harm your patterns have wrought, you can take bolt cutters to the chains of transactional niceness that have bound you for so long and instead experience the freedom of love when it isn't contractually obligated. That's the kind of powerful love that can transform the whole world.

FROM BABY STEPS TO BADASS PATTERN BREAKING

Sweet, *sweet* baby Two, I know looking inward and getting real about the gnarly resentment that's in there isn't your idea of a good time, but as they say in AA, what we resist persists. With your Heart Center tendency to attune yourself to something external, it's even more critical that you create the opportunity to intentionally look inward and reflect on what you really feel, not the sugary-sweet lies you tell yourself about how much you love everyone. I promise that when you lay down the armor of your good intentions, things worthy of love will be found within you. Let's take a look:

- Think of a person you're in relationship with that you give a lot to. If the first thing you feel when you bring this person to mind is a big rush of satisfaction, then the first question to ask yourself is, Are you satisfied with the relationship? Or are you just satisfied with how you feel needed in this relationship? Is it easy for you to let this person help you? What do you think will happen if you let them take care of you without you having to return the favor? Do you think that their reciprocity is on par with your giving? What does it feel like for you to receive from this person? Do you notice yourself giving more to them when you're feeling lonely or distant? How does always being the selfless, giving person in your relationships prevent you from being able to express your own needs in them? Under the warmth and satisfaction that you feel when you think of people you love, what other emotions are lurking?
- Now, this is going to run counter to your whole shtick, Nurturer, but I want you to turn your attention to your needs. Yes, the things that you spend a lot of energy pretending don't exist. What are you afraid will happen if you ask for something you need from someone you love? What are you afraid of feeling if you were to be honest with yourself about how much you need from your relationships? What would it take for you to trust someone to see your needs? What do you think it has cost you to stifle your needs? If you aren't allowing yourself to be fully seen and known in your relationships, how can you experience the love that you want everyone else to feel?

BADASS PATTERN BREAKING

Hey, Giver—how ya doing? I know you've taken a lot of flak for your ego structure, but before I tell you to change everything you're doing, I want to take a moment to acknowledge that everything you've been doing is going to be hard to quit—precisely because people *do* love how generous and selfless you are. I'm not asking you to stop being loving and supportive, but what I am asking you to do is to consider that being loving and supportive to others doesn't have to come at the cost of neglecting what you need from your relationships and from yourself. Here are some small shifts you can make to start extending the same care to yourself that you do to others:

- Someone you love is going to ask you for a non-urgent favor soon. The next time they do, give yourself twenty-four hours to consider if you really do have the bandwidth and energy to meet their need. Tell them you'll get back to them, and with the time that you're taking before giving them an answer, I want you to ask yourself if you're willing to do this favor without any expectations of something in return. If, and *only* if, you have the time, you have the energy, and you have the will to release any presumption that they should return the favor in equivalent measure, then you can say yes. If any of those three conditions aren't met, then kindly decline their request. Look at you, Two—you just held a boundary! Well done!
- There's a good chance that if you're not already swamped with obligations, you will be soon. The next time you notice yourself busy with a to-do list that's thirteen miles long, try asking someone you love for help. If they say no, then the good news is that you're going to get more practice asking for help. That's because you aren't going to stop asking for help just because the first person said no. I want you to ask someone else. Keep asking until you get a yes.

- Set a date and time every week that is exclusively for you to take care of yourself. Defend that time with the ferocity and tenacity of a vulture that just discovered all the smoked turkey legs at the Renaissance fair. Self-care isn't selfish, honey—it's necessary. Make yourself a priority, and free up space in your heart to give to others generously because you give to yourself just as generously.

TYPE THREE

Hall of Mirrors in a House of Cards

The shiny, mesmerizing disco ball is one of my favorite metaphors for the Type Three because I think it captures both the beauty and the suffering of Threes really well. A disco ball is a lot like the moon, not necessarily its own source of light but an incredibly effective (and beautiful) reflector of the light around it, casting everything in a faintly rainbow-hued shimmer. Much like disco balls, Threes can also reflect the light around them, mirroring the radiance and beauty of others and inspiring them to find their own inner light. Also, similarly to disco balls, Threes are made up entirely of tiny little mirrors that reflect the audience in front of them but really are just an attractive covering for a Styrofoam ball that is so structurally undeveloped that it crumbles under the tiniest bit of pressure.

In my work as an Enneagram practitioner, I've interviewed many a Three, and inevitably, the same thing ends up happening in our follow-up conversations. Once the Three has accepted their Threeness, shoulders slump, eyes lower, and the heaviness of their Three diagnosis presses its full weight on their resigned being. Shame is often the hardest to detect in this usually shamelessly self-promotional Type, but in the moment of their surrender to the knowledge of their true Type, it's impossible to miss. The experience of being truly seen for who they are, instead of what they do, is unnerving enough to unearth the question of whether they're worthy of love, which they're perpetually attempting to answer with productivity and external evidence of their value.

While the Three is famous for their chameleon-esque nature,

shape-shifting is hardly exclusive to them. In fact, in my opinion, Heart Center neighbors Two and Four aren't roasted hard enough for the litany of disingenuous disguises they rotate into and out of. Perhaps it's the ease with which the Three puts on and takes off the various personas they've constructed that earns them their reputation as the foremost shape-shifter on the Enneagram. Perhaps it's their attention to detail in creating their masks, often almost perfectly crafted to elicit that coveted praise from the individual in front of them, or perhaps it's just the sheer number of masks that won them this notoriety. Regardless of why, the Three is well known for their fluid form. And though they're unconvinced that they're deserving of love, they can rest assured that they are, at the very least, deserving of this little claim to fame.

Often referred to as the Performer or the Achiever, the Three is the mover and shaker of the Enneagram, wheeling, dealing, and taking care of business. They're identified by their impressive résumés and uncanny ability to make you feel like you're the only person in the room when you talk to them. Which is really quite darling until you watch them do the same damn thing with every other person in the room. Least obvious in their membership in the Heart Center, the Three is less emotionally expressive than the Two and Four, though their warmth and relationality are still hallmark features of this Type. The problem with this congeniality is that the Performer is so adept at morphing into a form that best suits their audience that it can be hard to tell whether the kinship we feel with the Three is genuine or is simply our own reflection mirrored back to us.

If it sounds like I'm being particularly hard on the Performers, it should be noted that Threes are one of those better-in-person Types. On paper, they sound like the sleaziest used-car salesperson on the New Jersey dealership lot, shamelessly hawking lemons like they have no moral compass or conscience. But in person, Achievers are charming, funny, and interesting, and honestly, they're really likable, despite all their shameless self-promotion. They have a natural confidence that wins people over and makes them feel seen.

The **Essential State** of the Three is **hope in a universal, benevolent, and creative force, outside their own efforts, that brings about progress.** This trusting foundation allows the Three to illuminate intrinsic value that exists. In other words, they reveal what is *already* present. They easily perceive what needs to be done, and they have the energy to do it, cultivating a better world by following through on the task that their intuition leads them to. Perhaps even more profound, the Three manifests value in the world by their ability to reflect back the natural value in others. They inspire others by mirroring the unique and treasured glow within each of us. Sounds hot as hell, right?

So, if the Essence of the Three is this sexy, why is it that the Three is the Type who is the most crestfallen and disgusted when they finally do accept their Threeness? Defeated by the realization that what they always suspected is now confirmed, they embark on a grieving process. They mourn the inner sense of secure identity that they neglected to build while constructing the rickety, cheap scaffolding of external praise and validation.

Well, aside from shame being their birthright by virtue of being a Heart Center Type, when the puzzle piece clicks into place and they can no longer deny their Threeness, the Three has to reckon with how much self-deceit and self-abandonment they've participated in, all in the name of impressing others. They've sold so much of their soul for the approval and acceptance of others that they aren't sure there is anything left to redeem even if they tried. And the prospect of trying something and then failing is haunting enough to keep them in an endless cycle of performing instead of introspecting.

Despite the bleakness that is the interior landscape of the Three, the super strength of this pretty but hollow Type is value. Specifically, the ability to bring value to every situation they step into, without having to do anything at all. Yeah, read that last line again,

Threes. *Without having to do anything at all.* I know that sounds completely made up, but stick with me here.

The substance at the heart of the Three suggests that regardless of what they do, or even if they do nothing at all, simply by being present, the Achiever contributes value to every situation. This is an absolutely buck-wild concept to the Three, who spends their entire life bouncing from one task to the next, hoping but never trusting that this next victory or accomplishment will finally bring them peace and inner security. The Three lives like they're a shark—if they stop moving, stop doing, stop producing, they'll die on the spot, starved of the main food group of their diet: other people's opinions about them.

Upon disconnecting from their Essential State, Threes look around the world and perceive it to be a place where they're only as valuable as what they're able to do and produce. And yet again, we find that a **Core Belief** rings at least partially true for all of us. We've all had the experience of internalizing a failure, falling into the trap of believing that **the quality, or lack thereof, of our work is somehow reflective of our very substance as humans.** If I'm being honest, I might have a *slight* soft spot for the Threes, because it's my opinion that their Core Belief—that identity and worth are tied to productive output—is one of the more challenging ones for us all to untangle ourselves from.

Threes look around the world and perceive it to be a place where they're only as valuable as what they're able to do and produce.

The Three can't resist the siren song of another project or challenge that they know will earn them praise and validation.

As they search for evidence for the Core Belief that they're already fully convinced of, the Performer's **Focus of Attention** is drawn to **whatever quick win they can tackle, some easy victory that only looks challenging** (if the Three had any actual doubts about their ability to succeed, they would avoid that challenge like the plague). The Three can't resist the siren song of another project or challenge that they know will earn them praise and validation, despite the project or challenge meaning very little to them. Of course, when they check the task off and make it look easy, they earn praise and validation, and boom—their belief is confirmed: They're loved for what they do, and who they are beyond that is of no interest.

The **Core Fear** of the Three is a fairly simple one: **the fear of failure.** Failing to complete a task, achieve a goal, or meet some measure of success is the phantom that the Three spends their life running from. They're convinced that one singular miss on their part will bring the meticulously curated house of cards they call a reputation—impressive and yet devastatingly fragile—to the ground in an instant. Just the absence of positive feedback on what they've accomplished is enough to activate their fear, sending them down a spiral of even more performing to overcorrect for the momentary lack of measurable success.

They're convinced that one singular miss on their part will bring the meticulously curated house of cards they call a reputation— impressive and yet devastatingly fragile—to the ground in an instant.

There's a degree to which we all fear failure, of course. Nobody likes to put forth their best effort and have to face the knowledge that it wasn't enough. But for the Three, who perceives the world as a place where love is strictly reserved for those who can demonstrate their worthiness in concrete terms, the fear of failure is all the more visceral. In fact, it's so all encompassing for the Three that slowing down or, God forbid, taking a break in between projects is out of the question. They'll throw themselves into the next project to soothe their angst about their own mediocrity.

The **Idealized Self-Image** that Threes combat their Core Fear with is the disco ball I referred to earlier. It's shiny, dazzling, constantly spinning, and ever shifting based on what stands in front of its mirrored surface. Threes fashion themselves into **busy little** worker bees with a penchant for stealing the spotlight, happy to put their heads down and work and even happier to bask in the external praise and validation that are offered in exchange for their work. They can't help but stand out—which creates its own kind of suffering that we'll talk about a little later—upstaging everyone with their ability to read their audience and offer them exactly what they're looking for.

If the Three is to ever have any hope of getting out of their patterns, the difference between this Idealized Self-Image and the Essence of intrinsic value is important to distinguish, because they can look pretty similar to the untrained eye. The Essential State of the Three is entirely free and unencumbered by the requirement that they work to make things happen or earn value through their efforts; their simple presence is enough to bring value and set the ball rolling toward a better world. The Three's intrinsic value is grounded in the solid earth of honesty and a sturdy sense of identity, knowing in an unshakable (but not cocky) way that they've got nothing to prove, baby.

The Idealized Self-Image, on the other hand, requires effort, and more than that, it requires calculation. In order to receive the assurance that they're deserving of love, the Performer must produce something valuable. It's transactional, and it requires that the Three somehow figure out what currency is useful to the person they're trying to impress. This external set of values becomes far more important than any internal set of ethics that exists within the Three—that is, if the Performer has spent any time identifying that code of personal ethics at all, which they usually haven't.

I know I'm being pretty heavy handed with Type Three's unstable sense of self, entirely built on the opinions of others. But it's crucial here to pause and remind ourselves that while the Three's internal center of gravity feels like a vacuum, their ego didn't develop in one, free from external messaging and rewards. They *have* earned love, praise, validation, and recognition for all their amazing accomplishments. They've been trusted with leadership positions, showered with awards, and promoted to titles that all feel like they reflect the value that the Achiever is hoping to be assured of possessing. So, as is true of all nine Idealized Self-Images, the mask of productivity and accomplishment the Three hides behind *has* helped them survive a world that does demand to see our résumés as proof of our worth. The first step in freedom from our Idealized Self-Image is recognizing it for the ways it was our life raft and how it got us to where we are today. Given how quickly a shame spiral can consume the Three when they reckon with the emptiness lurking behind their Idealized Self-Image, this reminder is all the more important for them in crossing the bridge from horrified humiliation to self-compassion for their survival strategies.

As long as they rely on external validation and criticism as the foundation of their identity, the Three's sense of self remains a perpetual construction site.

The ego wouldn't be able to stand on its own without some pretty hefty duct tape holding it all together, and that's where the Achiever's **Defense Mechanism** of **identification** comes in. **Identification is the practice of building one's identity out of the externals: results, achievements, and the praise, validation, and criticism of others.** As long as they rely on external validation and criticism as the foundation of their identity, the Three's sense of self remains a perpetual construction site, never achieving structural integrity. Identification perpetuates a cycle of selling themselves out in two key ways. First, because the Three is convinced that their selfhood is constructed with external materials, identification props up their Core Belief (work = worthiness), reinforcing the endless and panicked cycle of productivity and charm offensive. Second, identification amplifies the emptiness that reverberates from the cavity caused by their absent sense of self, haunting them with the knowledge that their projected self is constructed out of borrowed materials.

The **Vice** of the Three is **deceit**: bullshitting others and, principally, bullshitting themselves. In fact, **the Three deceives others precisely *because* they're deceiving themselves first.** The Heart Center Types are all always searching for their identity outside themselves, and this is the brand of dishonesty that fuels the Three's disingenuous song and dance.

The eternal identity crisis that the Three is constantly trying to resolve allows them to try on personas like they're shopping for a wedding dress. Wrestle the tulle and satin and lace into submission, clip it into place so it looks like it fits like a glove, come out and stand on the little pedestal, and listen intently for the subtle differences between the *oooohs* and *aaaahs* that different dresses elicit from their audience. Self-deceit creates the right internal conditions for the Three to fully commit to the bit and earnestly perform whatever character they've crafted for the audience before them in any given moment. The Three gets high on their own supply of delusions, but when the stage lights go off and they're left alone, they realize they've just shifted shapes for someone else's approval *again,* and the shame begins to sink in. The shame of being unable to stand on, or even contact, some solid ground within themselves.

Furthermore, self-deceit functions as the Three's response to their shame and nagging doubt about their own worthiness of love. It's hard to trust in the idea that they're deserving of love when the Performer doesn't even really know who they are. So, they overcorrect for this gap by applying their usual veneer of confidence, gaslighting themselves into trusting in the reaction of the carefully curated cast of characters they have at their disposal. With both the raw substance of their identity and the evidence of its value placed outside themselves, self-deceit answers their shame with an endless parade of meticulously decorated idols, fleetingly impressive enough to quiet the haunting echo of emptiness where the Performer's sense of self should be.

Let's not beat around the bush here: People who can't be honest with themselves generally don't stand much of a chance of being honest with others. So, the self-deception of the Performer tends to translate into deception of the people around them, all in service of preserving the image that they sell in exchange for the validation they crave and survive on. But the Three, being generally impressive at a number of things, has a lot in their arsenal of bad behavior and problematic patterns. Escalating friendly competition to an unnecessarily cutthroat new level, chasing the next achievement or title at the expense of their intimate and important relationships, and getting impatient and agitated at even the slightest slowing of progress are all on the menu too. Lying is just the start, baby!

Most of the time, their lies aren't premeditated or even that well crafted; they're just these knee-jerk reactions that fly out of their mouth before they've even realized the fib they've just told. Sometimes it's not even about covering their tracks so that their failures remain out of sight. Sometimes, in a sincere bid for connection, the Three will simply mirror the person in front of them, convincingly feigning heartfelt interest in the hobbies and interests of their audience, fostering a climate that feels more intimate than it actually is. This manufactured patina of closeness is perhaps one of the most harmful forms that their deception takes. In much the same way that the Three's identity is assembled out of equipment and hardware that aren't their own, thus lacking the necessary structural integrity to create something lasting, the foundations for their relationships are similarly laid on their performance of affection, not the slow and intentional process of growing real intimacy.

I don't often see it discussed in Enneagram literature, but another form of self-deceit comes up in Type Three panel discussions. While this one tends to be more painful for the Three than anyone else, it has external consequences and collateral damage all the same. Since Threes are naturally very gifted people, easily commanding attention because of their talents and charisma, people are drawn to this charming Type. But along with attention and affection come jealousy and ill will; others are envious of what the

Three makes look so easy. So as a means to avoid the painful experience of being the projection screen for other people's insecurities, the Performer will shrink themselves, dulling their natural radiance so as not to blind others. This particular deception is harmful to the Three simply because they're robbing themselves of an opportunity to be seen for who they are. An additional layer of harm in this performance is that the Three isn't doing anyone any favors by adjusting themselves for their audience's comfort. The Three can be a bright and powerful light for others to see their own value and inherent worth, but instead, by diminishing themselves, they reflect back the smallness and insecurities of the people in their audience. Radiant Threes, don't fall for their trap! Making yourself duller and less outstanding for the sake of others is relational malpractice. Take up space and blind 'em, baby! Let your light shine, because it's in your light that we can see our own most clearly.

Vanity is considered the mental fixation of the Three's ego structure, but it's also one of the most obvious things about them. The concern for how things look consumes the Performer, and it's oftentimes one of the easiest ways to distinguish them from other similarly task-motivated and competent Types. A common mistyped pair on the Enneagram are Threes and Ones; both are highly accomplished and high-producing sorts of people. When you give the same task to the Three and the One, both will get it done, and the results will even appear similar, but you'll need to take a second look to be able to distinguish who is responsible for which outcome. Upon closer inspection, the task completed by the One will be done with meticulous attention to detail. It'll be done the right way up to down, back to front, inside and out. When you take a look at the Three's work, it's going to seem great until you peek beyond the façade. You'll find that the whole thing is held together with gum and a shoestring. The integrity of their work is really none of the Performer's business so long as it looks good enough to get a little hit of validation.

The same vanity that drives Performers to cut corners and lie through their teeth also compels them to take a leave of absence in their relationships in pursuit of the next trophy to display on the mantel. Prone to workaholism, Threes have a nasty habit of phoning it in in their relationships, instead focusing their attention and time on concrete outcomes and deliverables. Relationships require honesty, which, as we've covered pretty extensively already, is one of the few things Threes aren't naturally good at.

Vanity is also the culprit behind the Three's routine of intensifying a little friendly competition into an all-out cage match; their ego capitalizes on an opportunity to flex their admirable chops at the expense of just having a good time. Fearful that losing even a silly, low-stakes game will tarnish their name, the Three lets their ruthless streak of aggression take over, charging onto the field with hostility and belligerence in defense of their image as a winner. The irony of the Three's brutally competitive streak is that it does more damage than good to their reputation, and they end up coming off as an antagonistic Canadian goose who can't just have a little light-hearted fun without taking it way too seriously.

The path out of all the lies doesn't take a genius to figure out. It's honesty. The honesty to look inside the echoing cavern within them and accept that if there are any values of their own in there, they sure haven't stuck to them. It's a devastating process for the Three to face the grim reality that they've spent their time and energy constructing idols for other people's praise, instead of contacting their own experiences and emotions to cultivate a sense of self that doesn't depend on what they're able to earn praise for. But in order for the external lies to end, the inner lies must stop first.

This **Virtue** of **honesty** for the Three is a practice of reflecting only what is true within them and pursuing action to bring forth only the things that are evidence of their *truthfully* held values. This necessarily requires the Performer to spend less time chasing after titles and trophies and instead spend more time figuring out what their values actually are. In other words, less mirroring others and more self-reflection.

Threes, this last section, going over all the ways you Dr. Frankenstein together some slick, crowd-pleasing prototype of a human being, has probably been a pretty rough thing to be on the receiving end of, so I commend you for still reading, here at the end of the chapter. We're in the home stretch, and I know you hate to abandon a task, so just stick with me a little bit longer.

Without having to lift a finger, you offer the world an incredible gift in the form of illuminating the inherent value that already exists within each person and each moment. Your simple presence sets a manifestation in motion because of the ways you're able to reflect the brilliance around you. I know it can be tempting and temporarily reassuring to see your value reflected back to you in awards and achievements, but you know as well as I do that the comfort these external markers of success bring is fleeting and ultimately unfulfilling. Your precious energy is so much better spent building solid ground within yourself than looking for it elsewhere. When you can let your true, whole self and the immensity of your light be seen without dimming it for the comfort of others, then those of us in your orbit will be able to see with absolute clarity what we're capable of.

Take a deep breath, Threes, and look around. Your whole world hasn't collapsed now that I've spent an entire chapter tearing down your façade and shining a bright spotlight on the ways that you bend the truth, deceiving yourself and us. I've said it to another Type, but that old saying about the truth applies to you too: The truth will set you free, but first it'll piss you off. If you've made it to the end of this chapter and you're pissed off at me or perhaps at yourself, then I've done my job—recognizing your honest emotional response is the first step. And now that all the ugly truth is out there on the table, your real work of truth-telling and self-discovery can begin. You've got this! I promise you can't fail now.

FROM BABY STEPS TO BADASS PATTERN BREAKING

Type Three, you're no stranger to to-do lists, agendas, and dead-lines, so at the risk of encouraging you into another productivity habit that doesn't always serve you, I'm going to offer you a new goal to aim for: the goal of cultivating a practice of *honest* self-reflection. These questions are intended to help you honestly and compassionately dig underneath the impressive and attractive fa-çade you employ and to give you clarity on the true substance of yourself, not the stuff that you've borrowed from the rest of the world:

- We've looked at how deceit is often more of a knee-jerk reaction in Threes than a calculated and well-crafted whopper intended to manipulate. Think back to the last time you witnessed a white lie fly out of your mouth before you had time to think about it. How did you want the other person to see you in that moment? And conversely, what parts of yourself were you trying to protect from being seen? What were you afraid would happen if the other person knew the truth? What do you think it costs your relationships when you aren't honest with others? What do you think it costs you when you aren't honest with yourself? Do you think your pattern of deceit plays a role in your experience of shame? What would happen if you began to see your reflexive misrepresentations not as some shameful secret but as some tender, less confident part of you desiring to be assured of its worthiness of love?

- Sweet Three, you have this tendency to put an enormous amount of pressure on yourself to achieve. Not necessarily for the sake of achieving, but in service of maintaining your image. This must take up a lot of energy. If you didn't feel the urgent need for external validation, what do you think you might have energy for? What could you free yourself up to experience if you weren't so preoccupied with impressing everyone else?

What have you sacrificed pursuing and exploring at the altar of everyone else's values? What if, instead of jumping into a performance when you begin to feel that need for immediate external reassurance, you viewed that feeling as an invitation to pause and find something within yourself that you value and deem deserving of love?

BADASS PATTERN BREAKING

Now, Three, I realize we've got to thread the needle here between offering you helpful practices that can shift your perspective and just assigning you another meaningless list of goals (that are based on *my* values, not yours) for you to achieve and update your résumé with. So, don't be afraid to fail. Thanks to your ego structure and the standard-issue terror you feel at the prospect of failing, missing the mark is still progress for you!

- A couple of years ago, all these think pieces were being written about how incredibly attractive it is when someone is gracious enough to let themselves be bad at something. I think it could be not only incredibly sexy but also incredibly *liberating* for you to let yourself be bad at something for once. Do it in front of yourself at first, and then, when you're really feeling courageous, let someone else see you be bad at something.
- The next time someone presents you with an opportunity that could result in an admirable outcome, I want you to give yourself twenty-four hours before you respond to their invitation. Take that time to consider whether or not the challenge, project, or goal is something that actually matters to you and aligns with what you value. If it does, then I want you to consider whether or not you've had enough time to recover from your last challenge, project, or goal. If the answer to that question is yes, then you've got one more standard to meet before you can accept the opportunity at hand. Ask yourself, *If*

I complete this project but no one ever recognizes or validates my efforts, will my confidence in my performance be enough for me? If you can't honestly answer yes, then do not pass Go, do not collect two hundred dollars, and enjoy a well-earned break, baby!

· When you catch yourself spinning tall tales about yourself, either trying to appear more impressive than you feel or, conversely, dulling your dazzle with false humility, take a beat, find some courage within yourself, and share a truth about yourself that you've been afraid to let people see. One of two things will happen: Either they'll connect with that sliver of your humanity, or if they don't, you'll have freed up that sliver from the grip of the shame that convinced you to keep it hidden in the first place.

TYPE FOUR

Feelin' Misunderstood
(and I'm Going to Make It Your Problem)

Take a scroll through the comment section of any of my Type Four posts (or, really, any Type Four–related post out there on the big, bad internet), and you'll find at least several Fours bemoaning how the memes about Type Fours are too reductive and couldn't possibly capture their terminally unique embodiment of their Fourness. To which I say, yeah, no shit, Sherlock. It's a meme, not a graduate-level dissertation. Much to the dismay of the Fours, they're not even special among the other Types in that regard. Every meme about every Type is reductive and oversimplified; that's kind of the point. But what is particular to Fours, as compared with the other Types, is that there is a deep desire within the egoic dumpster fire of the Four to be special, distinct, and significant.

Fours are a wonderful and necessary part of our world, reminding us that there is deeper meaning to be mined under the surface of our everyday experiences, bringing us back to the *why* in a way that helps push against existential dread and nihilism. Without Fours and the way that they show us the beauty of the world in how they allow it to move them, our daily lives would be bleak and barren. Fours' capacity to make significance out of the most somber of circumstances inspires hope sturdy enough to cling to as we weather the storms of loss and failure that inevitably come for us all.

Unfortunately, plagued by a sense of identity that is entirely constructed out of their perceived inadequacies, Fours spend a lot more time loudly lamenting what they believe is missing, rather than finding the abundance of meaning in the ordinary. Convinced that their incompleteness makes them impossible to love, they become self-absorbed, stuck in a prison of self-consciousness, comparing their insecurities with the highlight reels of the people around them.

This dramatized performance of their uniqueness is the Four's brand of Heart Center shape-shifting. They'll twist themselves into an undeniably special form based on the feedback they're receiving in the mirror that they've turned their relationships into. The Four dials up the volume on that which makes them unmatched by any ordinary schmuck, finding their significance in the reactions they get to their antics.

Fours are often referred to by the archetypal names of the (Tortured) Artist, the (Tragic) Romantic, or the (Insufferable) Individualist (okay, that last parenthetical qualifier might have been my own commentary). Fours have earned themselves the reputation of being the Enneagram's reigning drama royalty, moving through life with a distinctive theatrical flair, for better and often for worse. Particularly gifted at sensing deeper significance in ordinary circumstances, Fours offer the people they love a special experience of relationship and love, which is one of the reasons they've earned their moniker of the Romantic. Known for their vast emotional landscape and an innate creativity that goes far beyond typical artistic expression and touches everything they do, they can sometimes be one of the easier Types to identify in the wild.

Given their comfort with and appreciation for the full spectrum of human emotions, Fours have a beautiful gift for accompanying others into the depths of sadness, grief, and despair, offering presence and even steadiness in emotional darkness. Tormented by a fear that they lack a significant identity, though, they tend to spend much less time actually accompanying other people into the heart of their experience and much more time performing their scuba dive into their own emotional waters, searching for the most grotesque, oxygen-deprived sea creature as evidence of just how far down into the Mariana Trench they can go.

The challenging thing about roasting Fours is that any mean thing I could say about them is unoriginal to them, given that they've already thought of it and fifteen other rude things about themselves before lunch today. In part because they have a tendency to focus on what is missing within them and, not to yuck anyone's yum here, also in part because they just plain kinda enjoy the pain and get off on being misunderstood, the little weirdos are a bit more difficult to roast than most of the other Types. So, I'm going to have to try to enjoy this at least as much as you Fours; I think I'm up for the task, though.

Intense, moody, and volatile, Fours are more often known for their Tarzan-like emotional swings, careening between riding high on a dreamy fantasy of whatever is just out of reach and savoring the sweet tragedy of being unable to realize the delicious dreams of their own existential significance. Antagonistic toward any well-intentioned soul who attempts to cheer them up, Fours lament how misunderstood they are while rejecting those who get close enough to see them more fully. This whiplash exhausts the people around them, and people stop trying to understand them, only further fueling the Fours' conspiracy theory about how misunderstood they are.

Frankly, it's not that people don't understand the Four because the Four is so complicated and deep. If there is any misunderstanding about the Four, it's because they don't want to be understood, lest that understanding cheapen the unique and mysterious vibe they've cultivated. As much as they'll complain about not being understood, being misunderstood makes them feel different and distinct, which provides temporary relief from their fear that they aren't different or distinct.

The **Essential State** of the Four is **a deep sense of sharing in the complete connection between all things in the world,** and it grants them a unique gift in their ability to approach

The Four has such a uniquely beautiful capacity to give the people they love a special experience of being loved.

others and invite them to search beyond the surface level and find depth, mystery, beauty, and significance in the ordinary and mundane. By virtue of their Essential State, the Four has such a uniquely beautiful capacity to give the people they love a special experience of being loved. Unfortunately, as they, like every other Type (oh, look—another way you aren't special, Fours!), disconnect from their essential and original grounding of deep connection with everyone and everything, they begin to see the world as a place in which only those who are special, whole, and significant are deserving of love.

Their **Core Belief** that **this cold and lonely world has no love for the commercial, ordinary, or incomplete** drives Fours to reject everything within themselves that is commercial, ordinary, or incomplete. I've already used the phrase *terminally unique* in this chapter once, but it really is the perfect articulation of the personality that Fours craft for themselves and become overly attached to. Again, check the comment section of anything about Type Fours on the internet, and you'll see all of them vying to be the *most* unique among this already-offbeat Type.

If the Core Belief of the Type Four checks out, then a world in which love hinges on a person's ability to distinguish themselves from the crowd and ooze significance out of their every pore puts a lot of pressure on the Four to constantly perform their specialness. It doesn't leave them a lot of space to relax and be chill, considering they're moving around a world in which their very worthiness of love depends on the constant communication of that which is profound and significant.

Because the Four is in need of evidence that a missing piece of their uniqueness is waiting to be discovered in some incredible love story or profound life purpose, their **Focus of Attention** becomes fixed on **what is missing in the present moment.** In the newly-won-over crush that they've pined after for months, the Four finds the disappointing absence of butterflies in the relationship. In the brand-new shiny job that they've just relocated cities for, the Four zeroes in on how unfulfilled they feel by the new title or new digs.

In short, their Focus of Attention is on **the discrepancy between their romanticized fantasy and the reality of having the thing they thought they wanted, which only underscores for them that they're missing a piece of the wholeness that is required to be worthy of love.**

Because they're convinced that their worthiness of love lives and dies by their je ne sais quoi, the **Core Fear** of Fours can be plainly stated as **the fear of having no significance.** They fear that their existence ultimately has no special impact on the world and that they're just another basic-ass human being with nothing inherent to distinguish them (may as well hang up the LIVE LAUGH LOVE sign now, amirite, Fours?). Often mourning some phantom-limb-like absence within themselves—something seemingly lost long ago—Romantics fear that there is some fundamental piece of happiness hardware that was taken from them at some point early on. Now they must spend their lives trying to find it, usually in the inaccessible and unavailable. It's this fear—that the missing piece of their satisfaction and security is hidden in what they don't have—that results in their exhausting back-and-forth, push-pull pattern. This pattern romanticizes the person, job, relationship, or title that is just out of reach and then rejects the people, jobs, relationships, and titles that are available to them in the present. While every Type has a nasty push-pull pattern, Fours are particularly notorious for theirs, as it usually makes other people the collateral damage of their chase, catch, and subsequent dramatic release cycle.

Fours perform their uniqueness with flair, happy to amplify the reaction that people have to them.

If the fear that perpetually haunts Fours is that of being insignificant, then their **Idealized Self-Image** should be no surprise. It's that **they are the *most* significant, interesting, unique person to ever walk the planet.** They must possess the most emotional depth, the most creative perspectives, and the most unexpected of imaginations, and they need to make sure that everybody knows it. Fours perform their uniqueness with flair, happy to amplify the reaction that people have to them, whether that reaction is delight or disgust. In a small way, Fours are the embodiment of the old PR line that all publicity is good publicity. As long as people are talking about them, then they can be assured of their impact.

We're going to pause here to parse out the difference between the innate gift of depth and the performance of uniqueness that the ego produces when it's on its worst Idealized Self-Image behavior. The essential gift of the Four is a most finely calibrated attunement to beauty, mystery, and depth. Not to stroke your egos here, Fours, but that essential gift, the one that is innate to you, *is* special. It allows you to be present to pain and darkness and suffering, in yourself and in others, and to find something profound and meaningful in what could be otherwise experienced as bleak and desolate. An awareness that something more can be found in our suffering and pain is special in and of itself, without you needing to prove it. Good luck trying to convince the contracted Four of that, though.

On the other hand, the discount version of this beautiful Essence of attunement to significance is the ego's reproduction of it. It's a contrived and constant rendition of the Four's specialness, which sets them apart in all the ways one can be set apart. Lonely and insecure about the things they lack, the Four turns their pain into theater, dramatically wriggling out of the grasp of other people's understanding when they get too close to witnessing anything mass-market within the Romantic.

We're going to take a second pause here. This one is to remind ourselves that none of us construct and maintain these unwieldly, obnoxious ego structures just for funsies. These dramatic performances of the Four's uniqueness, their manufacturing of intensity and emotional chaos just to be seen as possessing depth? They *do* serve the Four's survival. The strategies employed by the Idealized Self-Image do make the Four stand out; they do create opportunities to bring their creative perspective to their world and make them impossible to forget, for better or for worse. For all the ways our Idealized Self-Image engineers our suffering, it undeniably helps us survive when our Core Belief and reality do occasionally line up. So, Fours, release your Idealized Self-Image with compassion and appreciation for the ways it has helped you get to the point where you no longer need it.

The great defender of the Four's special Idealized Self-Image is the **Defense Mechanism** known as **introjection**. For the Four, introjection is the construction of their sense of self using their deficiencies as the raw materials; it causes them to understand themselves entirely by what they believe they lack. **Introjection supports the entire ego structure by convincing them that the very core of who they are is defined by what they're missing.** Therefore, no matter what they have, that gnawing phantom-limb feeling of absence never leaves them, and they can't be satisfied by their current circumstances, accomplishments, and relationships. This Defense Mechanism also helps amplify the envy they feel toward others who seem to experience fulfillment in their lives, widening the gap between the Four and what everyone else seems to get to enjoy.

For the Four, introjection is the construction of their sense of self using their deficiencies as the raw materials.

Now is a great time to talk about the **Vice** of the Four: envy. Slightly different from the green-eyed monster jealousy, envy is that gnawing emptiness that one feels when they witness someone enjoying something that they don't possess. **The Four's envy makes sense when you consider how they understand themselves as being a big ole pile of their shortcomings; of course they're gonna pine for what they don't have.** This discontentment rattles around inside them, constantly intensifying their feelings of incomplete-

The Four is so defined by their envy that they can't afford to let anyone else be more special than them.

ness and the fear that their incompleteness will exclude them from being significant enough to be loved and fully seen. For all the ways they're gifted at making others feel special, the Four is so defined by their envy that they can't afford to let anyone else be more special than them.

Hungry for the satisfaction that other people seem to experience in their lives, Fours put the unattainable person, job, or home on a wobbly pedestal, convincing themselves that this missing puzzle piece is the long-sought-after key to their wholeness. When the unattainable person, job, or home eventually becomes attainable, Fours must face the disappointing reality that we all end up facing at some point: No singular person, job, or home will ever bring us completion. Completion is our work, and our work alone, and we can't outsource it.

Shame is probably closer to the surface and thus more obvious for the Four than for the other Types in the Heart Center. Turning the experience of being misunderstood into an entire personality, the Romantic laments the lack of intimate relationships in their life, all while conveniently failing to acknowledge the fact that they're often the architect of their loneliness. They chase people off before they have a chance to get close enough to truly see the Four beyond their curated façade of uniqueness. In response to their fear that they're insignificant, the Four's ego floods them with envy—an internal scowl at everyone else's contentment—and that externally focused envy allows the Romantic to at least feel significant in their experience of going without.

I'm tempted to go easy on the Fours here as we unpack some of their worst behavior patterns, because, in fairness to them, they do catch a lot of flak for the way they act in their relationships— maybe more than most other Types. But I don't think I'd be doing them any favors leaving them alone to sort through the way they blow up their happiness and ours. That's too likely to quickly devolve into some ash-rolling, clothing-rending, teeth-gnashing, self-referencing pity party. And anyway, I don't need to point out another thing they didn't get that everyone else did as further evidence of their incompleteness. Even if that thing is some harsh feedback about the way their self-absorption harms the people around them.

Threes and Fours both possess a competitive edge, but Fours are competing for a very different prize from Performers. Whereas Threes shift into sports mode in an attempt to be considered the best, the most valuable, or whatever superlative is relevant to the task they're engaged in, Fours are interested in one title and one title alone. The. Most. Special. Whether that is the most special friend, the most special lover, or the most special ex, the practical function of the role is less important than is its distinctness. Fours don't need to be the best you've ever had, but they do want to be the one that's impossible for you to forget.

Exactly how Romantics go about earning the designation of being unforgettable is generally a greatest-hits compilation of their worst behaviors. Having a particular penchant for pain and melancholy because of the irresistible allure of intensity, Fours aren't wrong to think that dramatic relationships tend to be more memorable. Unfortunately, this manifests itself in thrilling highs and devastating lows and an ultimately unstable and unpleasant experience of romantic partnership. You won't forget them, though!

Actual romance isn't the only stage for the Romantic's theatrics. This same battle can play out in just as ugly and exaggerated terms in the platonic and professional spheres as well. Cycling between heated pursuit of the attention of a friend or colleague and a sudden retreat from what felt like a promising friendship or work partnership, the Four stalks off bitterly to brood about how other people's recognition of their uniqueness doesn't quiet the nagging sense that they're missing something fundamental. The phrase *push-pull* is most often associated with Fours because of the emotional whiplash that the object of their current affection often ends up experiencing. The realization that this person or relationship was never the missing piece the Four has been searching for dawns on them, disappointment engulfs them, and they stiff-arm their just-previously beloved with as much ferocity as they put into their pursuit.

Fours can be reserved, but they don't always present as a withdrawn Type. They tend to be fairly loud and proud with their emotional expressiveness, but when the going gets tough, Romantics do pull inward, retreating into their big emotions, where they're safe to wallow in feeling sorry for themselves for all the things they lack. Self-aware Romantics will acknowledge that even though they can pretty quickly access and identify their emotions in the heat of the moment, the opportunity to step away and process allows them to gain clarity on what exactly within them is being triggered. They can feel freedom and lightness when they approach their big feelings as simply neutral information, not facts. Unfortunately, that takes time and practice, and because most Fours are comfortable in the realm of big emotions, they're usually happy to take emotions at face value. Then they run with the storyline that the initial rush of sentiments is constructing, which is generally yet *another* thread in their envious saga about how they're lacking.

A couple of Types on the Enneagram are diplomatically referred to as self-referencing, but diplomacy isn't my ministry, so I prefer to refer to them as having Main Character Syndrome. These Types believe that they're the protagonist of all of life and that they're the sun in the universe, around which everyone else orbits. While they come by it honestly (their natural envy fuels their delusion that there is some grand plot against their quest for wholeness), Fours do fall into this camp of Enneagram Types. They direct the conversation back to themselves regardless of the topic or the relevancy of their self-centering anecdote.

If it's any consolation, Fours, I feel uniquely qualified to speak about this particularly obnoxious pattern of yours, because I'm a representative of another Type that also assumes that the entire world is reacting to me. You know what? I just realized that my disclosure won't be any consolation to you, because it points out another way that you're not unique. . . . Oh well, too late now. But you see what I just did? I rerouted the entire conversation, which is supposed to be about you, back to the big, bad meanie of the Enneagram, Eight. See how annoying that is? *That's* what most conversations with you end up feeling like. The cost of all your self-referencing is twofold. Not only does it prohibit real connection, because it feels like we're always competing with you for the focus of the conversation, but it's also just *annoying*, and it makes us less likely to even *want* a connection with you when it seems that you're incapable of making it through a single conversation without being the nucleus of it.

For Fours and for the poor suckers they fall for, the path out of this volatility and exhausting back-and-forth is the **Virtue** of the Tortured Artist: **equanimity.** This is going to be a wild concept, Fours, but equanimity is a harmonious orientation toward the present, toward what exists right in this moment. In short, **it's the capacity to be content with what you *already* have.** Unlike the melancholy of your mental fixation, which longs for something you think you had in the past, and the emotional bender your imagination takes you on when you prop up the unavailable on a pedestal of false promise, equanimity accepts your surroundings exactly as they are—and finds a sturdy sense of satisfaction in them, without all the window dressing and adornment.

Can you even imagine it, Fours? Maybe I shouldn't encourage you to jump straight into imagining contentment, knowing your proclivity for creating an entire fantasy world in your mind, but whatever—the point still stands. You actually have the ability to experience satisfaction with your present circumstances and, perhaps even more crucially, with your present self. I know, I know—that sounds like absolute heresy, but stick with me here.

You're an absolute badass in your capacity to find deeper significance and beauty in the ordinary, possessing the ability to help others make meaning out of their lives, which throws people a lifeline in some of their darkest seasons. This is already a special gift; you don't need to distinguish yourself any more. Equanimity can support you through the waves of envy and frustration that will threaten to consume you when you have to confront the possibility that there is no existential meaning to your perceived incompletion. Equanimity can provide the reassurance that you've tried—and failed—to find in other people, in the perfect relationship, in the perfect job. Equanimity can provide something steady to hold on to and can keep your feet on the ground when your imagination wants to fantasize about the things and people you're pining after. Equanimity can remind you that what you already have—and, more importantly, who you already are—is complete enough to counter the narrative of envy and lack that your ego structure uses to send you on a wild-goose chase for your significance outside yourself.

All right, Fours, ya made it. We just spent an entire chapter talking about the thousand ways that you're exactly like every other Type Four on the planet. Now go out there, and actually do something different for a change: Find contentment with who you are, exactly as you are.

FROM BABY STEPS TO BADASS PATTERN BREAKING

You know, I used to date a man who would regularly and confidently declare, apropos of nothing, "I am *so* self-aware." It took all the self-restraint I had to not respond that there is a difference between self-awareness and self-absorption. Unfortunately for you, sweet Four, I'll practice no such self-restraint today. I know you spend a lot of time thinking about yourself, but that's not the same as observing and interrogating yourself in a way that makes you a better person. You have the capacity to dig deep; you just need a little help unpacking the ways in which you participate in your own melancholy. Here are some reflection questions to keep you honest:

- Four, we've talked a fair bit about the perpetual sense of longing that has convinced you of your incompleteness and compelled you to keep searching for the missing puzzle piece outside yourself. Combined with your tendency to romanticize the people, places, and positions just beyond your grasp, you set yourself up for inevitable disappointment every time you put someone or something on your pedestal. Thus far, your search for your missing piece in the externals has turned up empty, so what would it be like to abandon the search for good? What would it be like to get to know someone for who they are, without putting the pressure on both of you to find your completion in the discovery process? What if, instead of resigning yourself to identifying with your perceived deficiencies, you approached this phantom-limb sensation as an invitation to be present to what *is* within you right now?

- In a bid to overcorrect for your perceived shortfall and fueled by envy at what others seem to possess, you cobble together a persona that demands to be known for its uniqueness. What do you fear is at risk if you don't act special in your relationships? What would it take for you to trust someone to see what is ordinary about you? What do you think it costs you to maintain an aura of mystery at all times? How does always being the most unique person in your relationships prevent you from being able to enjoy what is special and unique about the people you care for? What if you recognized your desire to be seen as special for what it really is—a bid to be understood and connected with—instead of searching for the things that set you apart?

BADASS PATTERN BREAKING

Type Four, I want to advise you to start small here, but I'm all too aware of the fact that you don't tend to do anything small. That's exactly why starting small is so helpful. It's a shift away from your grand romantic gestures and dramatic productions. Not only that, but in another (helpful) affront to your typical ego structure, small shifts are *enough* to break your patterns. Here are some suggestions:

- I'm willing to bet there is some small, Basic™ thing about yourself that you keep buried deep—a guilty pleasure, if you will. Maybe you're a secret Swiftie, maybe you keep a countdown every year for the release of the pumpkin spice latte, or maybe you have your own pandemic sourdough starter that you began in April 2020, just like everyone else. The point is, find the little hobby or interest of yours that is so commercial and overdone that you would be mortified if people found out that you also love it, and let people see your unabashed affection for it. Give yourself the permission to have ordinary interests without worrying that their existence in your life threatens that which makes you an individual.

- Speaking of basic . . . start a daily habit of gratitude. Yes, I know, the lack of originality in this suggestion is massively offensive to you, my special little flower, but that's exactly why it's good for you. Not only that, but the envy and comparison that are regular features of your suffering keep you focused on what you don't have, so a gratitude practice will redirect your attention toward what you *do* have. This is a shift that will allow you to be more present and less fixated on feelings of inadequacy. Don't get too philosophical with this exercise. Every day, be specific in naming four or five people in your life, qualities that you embody, skills that you possess, and items or surroundings that bring you comfort and peace.

- Make it your mission to seek out that which is special and unique in the people in your life, without weaving it into the lore of your incompleteness. Challenge yourself to appreciate that which is distinct about another person simply because it's unique, not because you think this is the missing piece you've been seeking all along (it's not).

Part IV

THE HEAD CENTER

INTRODUCTION TO THE HEAD CENTER

Distinguished by their preference for intellectual activity, Fives, Sixes, and Sevens each have their own way of getting stuck in their heads. Sharing both an immense capacity for mental clarity and an equally immense capacity for anxiety, the Types that make up the Head Center are future-focused. Yet they suffer from a fundamental lack of trust in themselves, which then leads to them outsourcing their own agency to an external someone or something. Fives are the most obviously heady of the triad, immersing themselves in research and the pursuit of deep knowledge, often at the expense of human interaction and connection. Sixes can sometimes look the least intellectually grounded, simply by virtue of how quickly they can spiral out when their fear of the big, bad world ramps up. But their relentless preparation for the worst-case scenario and their endless interrogation of people around them are fueled by an active imagination that lets them envision what could go wrong. Sevens can appear more action-oriented than the other two Head Center Types, but that's only because they talk a big game of amazing plans they've dreamed up and want to pursue in the moment. However, they get everyone excited and on board and then abandon ship at the first sign of their own limitations.

The Head Center Types take in and interact with the world predominantly through their brains. In contrast to the big and intense energy of the Gut Center Types and the warm and fuzzy energy of the Heart Center Types, Head Center Types give off cooler, more rational, and sometimes more skittish vibes. They tend to always be on the move, either retreating to safety or chasing an enticing distraction. Analytical and alert, Fives, Sixes, and Sevens invite us to engage with what is empirical and to create something new with our current circumstances. On the flip side, Head Center Types also serve as a warning of the dangers of overthinking and getting trapped in our heads.

Here are some things that come naturally to the Head Center Types:

- a focus on the future
- a mental clarity that is precise and generative
- an insatiable appetite for more information, more opinions, and more options
- an angst about whether or not they'll be all right if they attempt to move forward
- a tendency to lack trust in themselves and give away their own agency by seeking security and safety outside themselves

As future-focused Types, Fives, Sixes, and Sevens have an amazing capacity to be visionaries and dreamers in the bleak landscape of the present, inspiring us all to work toward brighter horizons. With such an intense preoccupation with the future and such fast-paced, active brains, their ability to come up with something new can often lead them to find something to fear or at least project their mistrust onto. The fundamental questions that torment these Types are "Who can I trust?" and "Will I be okay?" This angst about taking the next step forward results in thinking and overthinking instead of action.

Fives, sensitive and sweet underneath all their intellectual prowess, fear the demands the world might make on them, not trusting their emotional capacity to withstand the intensity of those demands. Sixes suffer from a deep mistrust in themselves, but, terrorized by the notion that they can't trust themselves, they project that angst outward, perceiving threats around every corner and ulterior motives under every compliment they receive. Ultimately, they refuse to take any leap of faith, doubting their ability to face the demons of their own imagination's design. Sevens don't look afraid, but the endless brainstorming that they get emotionally high on becomes the web that they get caught in. They're frozen by all the possibilities they've dreamed up. And the fear that they may not choose the right dazzling one (and that the result may be more disappointing) keeps them scheming and spinning in place.

The Head Center Types are creative in how they take in information and synthesize it into something new. The Five's brain has the absorption capacity of a microfiber towel. They can soak up immense volumes of information, storing it deep in the archives of their technical and exacting minds, tinkering with knowledge until they can unveil new insight. The Six's brain has the superpower of impeccable observation, scanning the environment for all the often-overlooked particulars that may have import, then forecasting the safest and surest path forward. The Seven's brain is in the clouds, taking in reality and revealing the potential that waits patiently for the right time and touch.

That same creative, productive brain that allows Head Center Types to cook up some of the most novel, visionary dreams for the future is also the source of their hand-wringing and mental anguish, a hamster wheel that keeps them spinning without actually braving a step forward.

Fives, perpetually thirsty for more information and aware of the exact edges of their knowledge, never trust that they have enough information to make an informed decision, thereby locking themselves in a prison of endless research. Sixes, ever surveying the landscape for dangers, get stuck in a vicious cycle of threat assessment, preparing for disaster and never quite believing that they've prepared enough. Sevens, outwardly optimistic, are acutely aware that reality is disappointing more often than not. So they busy their minds creating fun escape routes to circumvent the letdown of witnessing the difference between what is possible and what is real.

Whether they're dreaming up new possibilities for adventure, connecting patterns that seem unrelated, or imagining the absolute worst-case scenario as though it's unfolding in real time, Fives, Sixes, and Sevens are particularly good at coming up with something brand new.

A particular brand of fear-fueled greed takes hold of the Head Center Types when uncertainty triggers their self-defensive patterns. That perpetually unsatisfied desire for more information, more contingency plans, and more choices is not the creative expression of a generative brain but an exhausting high-speed chase after peace of mind and confidence in a positive outcome.

The bottomless pit within the Five is a desire for more information, as though they're always a few cards short of the full hand needed to make the right call. The Five spends a lot of time gathering knowledge and facts. But haunted by an awareness of their limited capacity to know everything, they fear that what they didn't research or absorb in their data-collection efforts will reveal their incompetence. So they retreat further and further into their research-mode bunker, dawdling rather than deciding.

The endlessly anxious appetite of the Six is much more externally focused, scanning and rescanning (and again rescanning) their environment and relationships for any signs that precede disaster. Satisfied with neither the face-value information they're presented with nor their own extensive interrogation of it, the Six spirals out as they attempt to prepare more and more safety measures in advance of more and more unlikely outcomes that their imagination continues to come up with.

The Seven, perhaps the most obviously insatiable of the Head Center Types (hey, their Vice isn't gluttony for nothing), has a perpetual craving for more and more options that they can project their fantasies onto. The desire for endless choices doesn't appear fear-based to the outside observer, nor does it register as fear-based to the boredom-averse Seven. They're just trying to have a good time and live their best life (or at least that's how they'll rationalize it to themselves). But no possibility is ever quite exciting enough that it can't be usurped by another, and as the Seven continues to dream up more and more schemes and scenarios, they become paralyzed by the awful realization that there is no way for them to pursue all the amazing possibilities that they've already fallen in love with. The sucker punch that hits the Seven when they're already down is the fear that they won't make the right decision among all the options they've laid out for themselves. They'll have nowhere to run as the consequences of their poor discernment close in on them and they have to watch all of what could have been fade in the rearview mirror.

Head Center Types are an angsty triad, a cautionary tale about the dangers of relying too much on our powers of observation and analysis and not engaging enough with our emotional capacity, somatic wisdom, and will to act. When in a healthy place, though, the Head Center's intellectual clarity cuts through the destructive and controlling anger of the Gut Center Types and brings sobriety and steadiness to the emotional turmoil of the Heart Center Types. Their capacity to look at the present and make sense of what that implies for the future makes Head Center Types sound counselors, skilled troubleshooters, and inspiring visionaries who navigate through uncertainty with courage, calmness, and even optimism.

TYPE FIVE

When Intellectual Maximalism Meets
Emotional Minimalism

A little conflict-of-interest disclosure before we begin this chapter: I've gone on record many times to say that Type Five is my favorite of all the Enneagram Types. Don't let that fool you, though. I'm still going to expose you for the stingy, sensitive lil hermit crabs you are. Y'all are a pack of messy-emotion little weirdos just like the rest of us, and while I know it's probably more comfortable for you to be overlooked than be seen for how complicated you are, that's not how we do things around here.

Fives have a reputation for being quiet, curious, unobtrusive, and, to the untrained eye, a bit boring (they're not, but presenting as boring is a convenient camouflage in which to hide from the demands of others). Difficult to read and even more difficult to engage when things get hectic, Fives retreat into themselves when they feel imposed on, shutting it down before the chaos consumes them.

A guarded and placid surface conceals a roiling interior of intensity that exists within the Five. Their brain is constantly digging for more information as a means to understand their environment and relationships. While the pursuit of understanding is generally a worthwhile use of our mental energy, it should be noted that often the Five's search for comprehension is more of an attempt to establish a predictable pattern of behavior so that they can anticipate exactly how much this particular environment or relationship will cost them.

By virtue of their membership in the Head Center of Intelligence, Fives share in the dogged search for reassurance outside themselves. They give over all their agency and security to the information they haven't already consumed, and they set off searching for it, putting off a decision until they've gathered enough intel. But plagued by the anxiety that they don't have enough within them to meet the demands of the day, they never call off the search.

Often referred to as the Observer or the Investigator, Fives will sit back and watch their environment before (and often instead of) participating. They can be delightfully surprising, but that's largely because they're incredibly withholding of themselves and their inner world, so those of us who love Fives have learned to make a feast of the tiny crumbs of personal information that they sparingly disclose. Rich in knowledge, Fives can rely a lil *too* much on their intellect, feeding into a sense of superiority over people who present as more emotional.

Capable of some of the most precise and unique observations about things that the rest of us overlook, the Five has a brain that's a lot like one of those "grow a boyfriend/girlfriend/dinosaur" instant capsules. When immersed in information, the Five brain expands and expands and expands and then, out of nowhere, spits out something new—a fully formed and brilliant insight that takes us by surprise because we didn't realize how much was happening below the surface of the Five.

The **Essential State** of the Five is **trusting knowledge in the rhythm of life, which gives enough to each of us, granting them the intellectual superpower of clarity.** The Five has a steady, quiet, perpetually curious, and hungry intellectual capacity that loves to dive deep into research, knowledge, concepts, and experiences. The gift of this clear and precise mind is the Observer's generous, insightful, imaginative, emotionally lucid, and incredibly practical support of their loved ones. The Five brings composure to our nightmarish world.

The gift of this clear and precise mind is the Observer's generous, insightful, imaginative, emotionally lucid, and incredibly practical support of their loved ones.

When engaged with their sweet sensitivity and deep emotional capacity, they can be some of the most tender, loving people you'll encounter.

Of course, this tender, generous, helpful version of the Investigator is generally not how we experience them. In fact, the Five is often MIA and thus damn near impossible to experience *at all*. They come to the office, clock in, fulfill their assigned tasks, clock out, and retreat into their own little world—a world that their coworkers have no idea exists. They get home from work and withdraw behind the walls of their sanctuary, whether those walls are a home office, the chapters of a mentally stimulating book, or the practice of some skill they've been tinkering with for many years now. The strong boundary between work and personal life is as impermeable on the personal side as it is on the professional side. Partners, friends, and family members are often given a vague description of the Five's professional landscape, but nitty-gritty details of the day-to-day are hard to extract from the closed-off Observer. Colleagues may know even less of the particulars of their personal life, which works just fine for the guarded Five.

These rigid barriers and their tight-lipped approach to the world are the predictable outcomes of the **Core Belief** that Fives hold: **The world is an overwhelming, bossy, intrusive place that takes much more than it gives in return.** And as is true of every Core Belief of every Type, Fives are right! We've all had the experience of being half-asleep at the wheel, depleted from what seem like endless demands on our time and energy, wondering when the hits are gonna stop coming. Fives feel like the hits never stop coming, their tender little nervous systems on the constant edge of overwhelm.

If Fives believe the world that surrounds and consumes them is one that demands more than it returns, their **Focus of Attention** is on the dementors in their world: **vampires.** These vampires take the form of other people, their responsibilities, and their own emotions, and might flood Fives to the point of sinking the rickety little rowboat they're working furiously to keep afloat. Fives spend a lot of time budgeting out their energy and emotional resources, carefully earmarking what they think they'll need to get through the day until they can retreat into their internal world to recharge. Mindful of the anticipated start and end times of their engagements, Fives show up and give what is expected of them and then disappear when more than was planned for is required. Unexpected intrusions bring unexpected demands, providing Observers with more evidence for their belief that **the world is just one giant, imminent emotional avalanche waiting to engulf them.**

Focusing their attention on all the things that could consume them confirms their belief that the world is a formidable place and sows in them the sense that they could be overtaken at any moment. Simply put, the **Core Fear** of Fives is **being exposed as flustered, ineffective dum-dums.** Researchers fear that even a momentary lapse in their lifelong self-sufficient posture will open the floodgates to the demands of others and reveal not just their incompetence but how pitifully low their threshold is for overwhelm.

Researchers fear that even a momentary lapse in their lifelong self-sufficient posture will open the floodgates to the demands of others.

Fives spend their lives collecting information and guarding their energy and the limited internal resources they have, staving off others' unpredictable emotions and requests. Always aware that there is more for them to learn, Fives often withhold the extent of their expertise. They fear that if they share their knowledge, they'll be subjected to a pop quiz, and the limits of their research and knowledge will be exposed by someone who knows more than them. More sensitive than they let on, Fives are unconvinced that they won't be consumed by their own emotions, let alone the emotions of others, so they opt to do their best to remain distant from both external and internal sources of emotion.

Fives starve themselves of material and affective entanglements and instead feast on the sense of superiority afforded to them by their threadbare existence.

In response to the world that they experience as overwhelming and in defense against the possibility that they'll be blindsided and overpowered by a sudden gust of unanticipated emotion, the **Idealized Self-Image** emerges as a way to survive. It looks similar to Fives' Essence at first blush, but upon closer inspection, it amounts to only a B-rated version of it. Their Idealized Self-Image is **a self-sustained ecosystem—an intelligent and remote island of a human being, safe and isolated from the taxing requirements of being in relationship with others.** They pride themselves on how little they've learned to survive on. Fives starve themselves of material and affective entanglements and instead feast on the sense of superiority afforded to them by their threadbare existence.

For the Five, it's so important to be able to recognize the difference between their essential gifts (clarity and precision) and the counterfeit imitation produced by their ego (stubborn self-sufficiency and minimalism). Clarity and precision come from a quiet, calm mind that observes its surroundings with receptivity and openness and from an ability to respond to an unpredictable environment with generosity and sensitivity. When they're in their Essential State, that clarity and precision are generative, creative, and unencumbered by a fear of looking stupid; the Five enthusiastically delights in the unfolding process of discovery rather than being attached to a factually sound outcome.

Self-sufficiency and minimalism, on the other hand, are guarded stances. The Five stiff-arms the mutuality of relationships, dodging the kind of affective overwhelm that can well up in us when we allow ourselves to be moved by the outside world. Self-sufficiency is the Five's brand of rejection; they contemptuously refuse to imagine that closeness and intimacy with people could be a source of support instead of suffering for them. Minimalism, be it material or emotional, is a self-soothing strategy. It allows the Five to rationalize an aloof stance toward people that will deplete them and toward things that feel temporary in a cruel and backbreaking world.

If this is getting overwhelming, sweet Fives, let's take a quick minute to come up for air and remember why we commit to performing the bit that is our Idealized Self-Image. We're not just doing it for our own entertainment, after all. No, we find ourselves caught up playing the role of our Idealized Self-Image because it helps us navigate an exhausting, demanding world and get our needs met enough to soldier on another day. Fives enjoy solitude as a reward for their self-sufficiency; they're trusted for their expertise; they're invited into complex problems because people know that they won't complicate matters more. This Idealized Self-Image is not only a façade but also a shelter for you in a chaotic, intrusive world, and emerging from behind it for good requires compassionate understanding as to what sent you hiding there in the first place.

The **Defense Mechanism** of Fives is often referred to as **isolation**, although if you've ever been on the receiving end of a Five's defended state, quite frankly it's more offensive than defensive. While their Defense Mechanism does isolate them, they frame it as compartmentalization. Fives defend their self-sufficiency by dissecting their emotions

By disengaging from their emotions and relationships, Fives can avoid being overwhelmed by them.

from their relationships, placing their feelings for someone outside the equation, all so they can more easily defend their castle by warding off icky feelings of fondness, care for others, and closeness. By disengaging from their emotions and relationships, Fives can avoid being overwhelmed by them.

Isolation is particularly useful as a Defense Mechanism for Observers because it's a passive way for them to regain control. **If they can't be reached, they can't be depleted of their resources or energy, and they can meter these out (or not) according to their**

agenda, not someone else's. It also supports their delusion of self-sufficiency by sequestering their feelings in real time—out of range of the support, love, and understanding that others can offer them, forcing them to survive the waves of emotion on their own. While, yes, isolating themselves from the demands of the world guards them against overwhelm, it also proves them right that they can't handle it. So until new, contradicting evidence is provided, the cycle continues.

Fives' greed comes in the form of panic-hoarding alone time and other emotional resources.

The **Vice** of Fives is known as **avarice**, or, if you're not a regular reader of the thesaurus, greed. It's not a greed for things, though. Fives are famously minimalistic in their life-style, often obscuring material wealth behind the cheap camo print of simplicity. Instead, **it's a greed for the resources that they believe will prevent them from being overwhelmed—time, space, energy, and information.** Fives' greed comes in the form of panic-hoarding alone time and other emotional resources to guard against unexpected intrusions and demands; they're preemptively stingy, closed-off cheapskates with their inner world. Fives refuse to give to or take from the external world lest it move them or reveal standard-issue human incompetence in them. Their avarice is both the experience of and the fuel of the fear of being caught without enough.

Overwhelm activates the hangry avarice of the Five in that it threatens to excessively tax the already-anemic luxuries that they allow themselves to enjoy. This causes the Observer to fear that all their emotional downsizing has left them without enough rations for a harsh winter of unexpected demands and external expectations. Since they're convinced that their instinct to stockpile is in response to an accurate inventory of diminishing resources, their Vice further justifies their miserly allocation of their time, their affections, and themselves.

Observers play their cards fairly close to the vest, so the fact that they're as timid and easily startled as they feel isn't always immediately obvious to the casual bystander. Their withdrawn tendencies generally mean their experience of anxiety is inward and much quieter. It's both isolated and isolating as a result of their instinct to wall off at the first sign of intensity and chaos.

The Observer battles a particular brand of Head Center fear: an anxiety around not having enough to fare in a disorderly world, regardless of the fact that they've been the architects of their impoverished emotional connections and lack of creature comforts in their bid for self-sufficiency. Rather than brave the task of connecting with others as a means to enrich themselves, the skittish Five buries their head in the sands of research and mental exploration, where they think they'll eventually intellectualize themselves out of their dread. Much like the way the entire population of the United States started panic-purchasing toilet paper at the start of the Covid pandemic, the Five's response to the fear of an uncertain future is to hoard what they think they'll need in order to hunker down and survive.

We've given an awful lot of airtime to the pain that their ego structure inflicts on the Five, but as someone who has dated many an Observer in my romantic career, I think I'm uniquely qualified to speak on just how much pain their ego structure inflicts on the rest of us (not that being uniquely qualified to talk trash about only one Type is going to stop me from talking trash about the rest of them). In any case, for all the people who have attempted to get close to this cagey Type, let me bear witness to *our* pain now.

Speaking of dating, if you've ever braved the online dating space (or maybe even if you haven't—people have a lot of audacity these days), you've likely experienced being ghosted, had the rug pulled from underneath your sweet little trusting heart just when things were getting good. That . . . that is some Five shit.

Now, I'm not saying everyone who has ever ghosted anyone is a Type Five. There are conflict-avoidant cowards representing every Type on the Enneagram, but the sudden, swift disappearance is a pretty premium example of how a terrified Five might withdraw from anything they perceive to be threatening to overtake them. Slipping silently into the night, burrowing into the safe predictability of their own isolation, these emotionally thrifty Types will retreat until the storm has passed and the intensity has died down.

As someone who can often benefit from a little cooldown time before engaging in conflict, I'll be the first to acknowledge that withdrawing from the heat of the moment is sometimes the more constructive path forward. The key to taking a step back, though, is communicating before fleeing the scene, and that's the crucial step Fives usually bypass. Since they opt to vanish without a word and reappear only when cooler heads prevail, the damage is already done by the time Fives feel ready to engage with the issue. Sensitive lil Observers, I know retreating into your shell when things get heated feels protective and safe, but it comes at the cost of giving yourself irrefutable proof that you actually can survive intensity, conflict, intrusion, and even overwhelm. As long as you keep running away, you'll never get to catch a glimpse of exactly what you're made of.

One of the most obnoxious behavior patterns of the Five just so happens to also be the mental fixation of their ego structure: stinginess. The Five's stinginess is distinct in that it's the withholding of what they've been hoarding. This can look like financial and material withholding, as well as secrecy and an aversion to taking an emotional risk in their relationships. It can be as simple as buying an impersonal gift for a loved one because they don't want to risk looking stupid by attempting to get something more and missing the mark. Or it can look as buck wild and audacious as having multiple "intimate" relationships, all void of actual emotional intimacy, of course.

Even when they aren't being unethically non-monogamous, Observers do prefer to operate under stealth and secrecy, keeping away from people's prying eyes and intrusive lines of questioning. Secrecy, much like pretending to be boring, is a handy veil for

Fives, keeping them under the radar by not attracting anyone with hints of inner intensity. Staying out of sight and keeping their movements under cover also helps them maintain the lie that they don't need anyone else, because they're not letting anyone else in! In short, their covert approach to life serves a number of functions for their ego structure, helping them stay in their stingy and sneaky little patterns.

Yet another hallmark of Type Fives is their chilly aloofness. They present with a signature cold front, impersonal and curt, and even more so with people they already know than strangers. This nonsense is their way of keeping the people they care about, who have the power to move them, at arm's length so that no one can surprise them with an unanticipated demand that they're unable to meet. Guarding themselves against unexpected overwhelm, the Five can go frosty on a dime, warding off people with their sudden lack of interest. In short, they go on the offensive with their icy façade so that they won't have to go on the defensive while feeling overwhelmed.

The **Virtue** of Fives is **non-attachment,** and I think it's one of the Virtues that requires the most unflinching self-honesty. Fives can easily delude themselves into thinking that their defensive posture of isolation is actually non-attachment. Spoiler alert: It's not. Let's get into what the Virtue of non-attachment actually looks like on the ground.

We've got to remember that the Virtues are somewhat of an antidote to the Vices. They're to be intentionally cultivated as a way to mitigate strain and suffering at the hands of an active ego structure. **Non-attachment, as it relates to the expanded emotional capacity of the Five, is a relaxed, open posture to their resources, allowing them to trust that they have enough already and don't need to clutch their little luxuries like someone is trying to take them away.** Non-attachment in the Observer is a grounded sense of security that their tender little hearts have enough and are enough to survive in this chaotic and overwhelming world. Non-attachment challenges the Five to release their grip on their stock-piles of emotional rations and take a more honest approach to assessing what they actually need in order to meet demands, whether or not they were anticipated.

Fives, y'all have skated by with a reductive reputation for being logical little robots for too long, and I think y'all like it that way. It keeps people outta your business if they think there isn't much business in the first place. But you and I both know better than that, and it's time to let the world see just how weird and wonderful you are.

The gift that you offer the world, when you're being your eccentric, quirky, unguarded self, is a mental clarity that is both precise and creative, generating brand-new insights from the information you take in as you observe your surroundings. You give the rest of us new ways to think about things, and your ability to see things and find brilliant, clear, fresh insights is exactly the thing we need in a world that seems to have increasingly complex problems. I know that the world is ravenously demanding and that your sensitive heart is more easily moved than you want to admit. But we both know that there is so much more under the surface than you let on—intensity, vision, and a capacity for deep understanding that is sourced from your inherent tenderness. Not only do you have more than enough to face the world, but you also have more than enough to give to the world, without ever running out.

All right, you quirky little weirdos, despite your best efforts to hide and resist being exposed, we made it to the end of the chapter, and you're still alive! Maybe you're feeling a little overwhelmed, but I promise it'll pass, if you let it. Take a minute if you need to, but I know you're more than capable of meeting the demands of this challenging world. Let us get to know you for the delightful package of eccentricity and unique perspective that you are.

FROM BABY STEPS TO BADASS PATTERN BREAKING

I know, I know, Type Five—you just finished reading your chapter, and I'm going to ask you for more. I'm so demanding! You're probably exhausted, sweet Five, but I promise you can make it through a few hundred more words. And you, more than any other Type, have the intellectual hardware for self-observation. It's just a matter of trusting that you also have the emotional hardware to face whatever you're confronted with when you turn your well-practiced skills of observation on yourself. Here are some questions to show you what you're capable of:

- Much of our examination, sweet Observer, has been centered on how you seem to exist on the perpetual edge of overwhelm, guarding your delicate heart from being consumed by the insatiable appetite of the world. Can you approach your fear of overwhelm with curiosity instead of dread for a moment, dear Five? What are you afraid might be revealed if you're caught off guard? What do you think might happen if you allow someone to witness your tenderness? What do you think is the cost of your compartmentalization? What if this innate sensitivity of yours is not a liability at all but the port of deep understanding within you that provides connection and safe harbor for others who feel similarly small and ill-equipped to withstand the uncertainty of their lives?
- A manifestation of your suffering, Type Five, is your angst about not having enough within you to survive the demands of intimate relationships and daily life. This fear leads you to patterns of both panicked stockpiling of what you think you'll need and closefisted emotional stinginess that further isolates you from the relationships that you worry will drain you. What do you think this relational frugality has cost you? These efforts take up a massive amount of emotional energy and mental vigilance. What do you think you might have space

and clarity for if you didn't try to soothe your fears by constantly running to restock your underground bunker of emotional provisions? What if you gave yourself the chance to see that closeness with others can be restorative instead of depleting? And what if, in the experience of receiving renewal in your relationships, you also gave yourself the opportunity to see how much you have to give toward the renewal and resourcing of others?

BADASS PATTERN BREAKING

I know you love a good mental exercise, sweet Investigator, but it's time to take it from theory into practice, okay? Come on down from your ivory tower, and take your first wobbly baby steps into a new way of being. I promise you that you already have everything you need to free yourself from your old patterns. Except, of course, for the new data set that these small experiments will provide you with. I think that once you run the numbers, you're going to find that you really are more capable than you've given yourself credit for. Here are a few suggestions to take for a trial run:

- Participate in some group activity in which you have zero expertise. Maybe go to a themed trivia night that centers on a TV show that you've never seen, or tag along with friends to a hobby of theirs that you've never tried. Let yourself be seen totally out of your element, without the armor of your usual intellectual prowess. If you get frustrated, all the better. Let your friends see that too! Stay present to what comes up for you, and let others accompany you in this unfamiliar territory.
- Let someone waste your time. Sounds like hell, I know, but stick with me here. Your time is one of the places where you're predictably guarded, so it's a perfect place to try something new. Commit to spending time with someone without an agreed purpose, agenda, or wrap-up time. If this feels too

daunting, start small. Stay until the very end of a party you were invited to in order to help clean up. Give yourself the chance to see that occasionally you can survive with softer boundaries around your time.

· The next time you're feeling totally drained or overwhelmed, reach out to someone you trust and let them show up for you. When things get stressful, sweet Five, you have this tendency to lean really hard into your pattern of stubborn self-sufficiency, shutting yourself in until the pressure subsides. Letting someone in with you and letting them witness and accompany your sensitivity will give you new perspective on how your relationships can actually be supportive and sturdy, instead of demanding and draining.

TYPE SIX

Who Needs Trust When I've Got Projection?

As I was considering how to begin this chapter, I had hoped to present the Six with enough clarity and honesty to avoid triggering either their general disdain of flattery or their underlying suspicion that everyone hates them. Then I realized I was setting myself up for an impossible task, so I'm just gonna rip the Band-Aid off and trigger away. Much as they suspected, the Type Six is rather divisive in the world of the Enneagram. People either love them or truly, truly hate them. Loyalty, trustworthiness, and an offbeat sense of humor all work in the Six's favor, earning appreciation from those of us who love them. But on the other hand, their relentless questions, utter unwillingness to trust in most everything around them, and laser-like focus on the worst-case scenario can run our patience thin and our tolerance low for this fearful Type.

Sixes can be easy to spot, their anxiety launching them into an interrogation that any bad cop in a good cop–bad cop duo would be proud of. Generally suspicious of anything they're told and particularly suspicious of any compliments they receive, they want to test everything for the hidden agendas and ulterior motives underneath. When they can't quite figure out what the self-serving motives of the people in front of them are, Sixes embark on the project of trying to anticipate them, imagining every outcome that points to their demise. Stubbornly pessimistic, they refuse to imagine that things could work out for the best, and they have a particular knack for forgetting all the crises that they managed to survive in the past. In fact, Sixes are notoriously excellent in the heat of a crisis, intervening with precision and strong instincts, their heavy-handed focus on preparation serving them and others incredibly well. After the crisis event is behind them and everyone is safe and accounted for, they completely forget how well they navigated the moment and go back to fretting about their capacity to handle emergencies and plot twists.

Sixes belong to the Head Center of Intelligence, along with Fives and Sevens, and they're perhaps the most unambiguous in their relationship with fear and mistrust in themselves. Sixes don't trust anything or anyone at first blush, and they're gonna let you know about it. Far louder than Fives and far less optimistic than Sevens, Sixes seek reassurance outside themselves in their threat-assessment planning and in the loyalty they expect in return for their stubborn allegiance to arbitrary rules, institutions, and people.

Sixes are often referred to as the Loyal Skeptics, Guardians, or Devil's Advocates of the Enneagram. These three archetypal titles all touch on distinct features of Sixes, which include their unwavering, ride-or-die, Bonnie-to-your-Clyde, bordering-on-stupid loyalty to the very few who have earned their trust. They employ a rabid-raccoon-like ferocity with which they protect the few things and people that have earned their trust. And they walk under an obnoxious, self-assigned thundercloud, raining on the parade of everyone else's arguments and proposed plans. They poke holes in ideas and suggestions, revealing how vulnerable even the best options are to the worst-case scenario, should it come to pass (oh, and it *will* come to pass).

What is fundamental to understand about Sixes is that they perceive the world as an inherently dangerous place. Threats to safety and security lurk around every corner and in every alleyway, and the worst-case scenario isn't just possible—it's *imminent*. I say that's the fundamental thing to understand about Sixes, but they'll never let you forget that's how they see the world. As a particularly expressive Type, Sixes rarely STFU about their concerns and fears. They're worried, and you need to know about it so that *you* can do something about it (and then they won't have to face it themselves).

They're a calm and courageous pilot through stormy waters and uncertainty to a safer horizon.

It's not all bad with Sixes, not that they'll believe me on that. Their **Essential State** is a place of **unshakable faith in themselves and in the rest of the world, that things will be all right.** From this trusting place, Sixes, at their utter best, embody devotion, a grounded love for their people, and guidance. They're a calm and courageous pilot through stormy waters and uncertainty to a safer horizon, a sturdy and steadfast presence when their loved ones are facing a crisis. This is why Sixes make some of the best partners and most dedicated team members. They truly commit themselves to others, and they're able to troubleshoot and navigate to stability and security. These gifts are necessary and beautiful to the relationships that Sixes engage in. Unfortunately, these gifts cease being gifts and turn into primitive survival strategies when Type Six's Core Belief begins to distort their vision.

The **Core Belief** of the Loyal Skeptic begins to take shape as they look around the world and observe unpredictability, hazards, and malevolent forces at work, and they ultimately reach the conclusion that the world is fundamentally unsafe. **Not only is the world dangerous, but people are also only looking out for themselves.** And in all fairness to the Sixes . . . are they wrong? Life is fragile and short, and all the evidence we need to prove this statement is just a doom scroll away on the social media app of your choice. The world *is* a dangerous place, and certainty is a flimsy delusion that we all attempt to soothe ourselves with.

With the particular perspective that the world is a dangerous place, the Six's **Focus of Attention** is on **everything that could go wrong in any given moment.** When the Six walks into the room, they've already clocked the emergency exits and begun to mentally run through plans A, B, and C if those emergency exits all become blocked. Their Focus of Attention serves to unearth evidence for the working theory that the Six is already sold on—that the world is unsafe and even kind gestures conceal hidden agendas and ulterior motives. By seeking out and focusing exclusively on threats, the Six is able to build a solid case that the world is indeed a scary, horrible place, even though they had already reached that verdict.

The **Core Fear** that runs a Type Six's blood ice cold is that, in this dangerous world, they're utterly helpless to protect themselves and the ones they love and that **all their preparation and vigilance will never be enough to keep them and their loved ones safe.** The source of their mistrust can be difficult to see clearly because the Six doesn't appear to be mistrusting of themselves; they appear to be mistrusting of *you* (and everyone else— though it's not personal, Sixes will make it

The Core Fear for the Six is not of the big, bad, scary world but of their own inability to survive and protect their loved ones in the big, bad, scary world.

feel that way). We'll talk about that later (a lil foreshadowing for ya there—a Six's favorite dramatic device). But for the time being, the takeaway here is that the Core Fear for the Six is not of the big, bad, scary world but of their own inability to survive and protect their loved ones in the big, bad, scary world.

So this is where those beautiful gifts of devotion and guidance become twisted into self-defensive strategies for survival, and the **Idealized Self-Image** of the Six emerges. **The Six wants to be seen as loyal to ensure the loyalty of others.** Also, the Six wants to be seen as prepared—so that they're always ready for the disaster waiting in the wings. Their lack of trust in themselves is clearly re-

They're loyal because they crave others' loyalty—while constantly testing the trustworthiness of others' loyalty.

vealed by their Idealized Self-Image. They're loyal because they crave others' loyalty—while constantly testing the trustworthiness of others' loyalty because they don't trust themselves to pick the right people to be loyal to.

The difference between devotion and loyalty is really important to note here if a Six wants to be able to interrupt their ego structure when it gets activated. When a Six is devoted, there is a level of trust in the relationship because they trust themselves enough to discern that this relationship is worthy of their time, attention, and efforts. They trust themselves to know that the relationship is safe, and they trust the other person to be faithful to them, not needing to grill them just to be able to accept their word.

Loyalty, though, when employed as a strategy by the Six, is transactional. The Six is loyal to people and institutions because they want their people and institutions to shelter and protect them. (Say it with me again: *because the Six doesn't trust that they're able to shelter and protect themselves.*) Because the Six views loyalty as transactional, a type of currency, they can't trust in it. So, when someone else comes along and has something much more valuable to offer the people they're hoping will protect them, the Six will find themselves in a really compromising position.

We can see the same contrast when looking at guidance compared with preparedness. Guidance relies on an inner wisdom and clarity, trusting in their ability to respond in the moment, whereas preparedness is mental angst spent anticipating and trying to mitigate circumstances outside the Six's control. Because, as is always underneath the Six's anticipatory angst about what is up ahead, they don't trust themselves to be able to respond in the moment without airtight preparation. But because the foundation of trust in themselves is missing, the Six doesn't trust their exhaustive preparation efforts either.

The Six spins away on the hamster wheel of anxiety, frantically running themselves around and around as they imagine and prepare for the worst, all while doing everything they can to avoid it, and they don't end up making any progress. No preparation is enough, and immobilized by their fear, the Six denies themselves valuable opportunities to see the evidence of their own capacity for survival. So their fear goes unchallenged, and their avoidance or belligerent interrogation (depending on the situation) persists.

If it feels like we've been going around and around in a circle and you're getting dizzy and disoriented, sweet Six, it's because we are. So let's take a little break to gain some perspective on this vicious cycle and find out why you would even stay on the ride if it's so miserable. All of us put so much effort into maintaining our Idealized Self-Image because it's actually pretty effective at getting us through the day. Six, you're appreciated and loved because you're the one who knows to bring both Tylenol *and* Advil (and sunscreen and Band-Aids and an extra pair of socks and snacks). You win people over by being belligerently loyal to your chosen people. Your skepticism and pessimism guard your anxious little heart against disappointment, because you never got your hopes up in the first place. This front of cynical readiness and aggressive allyship *has* been successful at protecting you, sweet Six, from the tumult of the world. It's okay to extend understanding to yourself for why you thought you had to be who you thought you had to be.

The **Defense Mechanism** of the Six is known as **projection: the casting of their own inner mistrust onto their entire external environment.** Projection as a Defense Mechanism operates sort of like that ole trope in horror films. The phone keeps ringing, and the voice on the other end is threatening and ominous, until it's revealed toward the end of the movie that the call has been coming from inside the house all along and the true horror is lurking in wait, the final bloodbath imminent. For the Six, projection is dependent on two simultaneous illusions. First, that the threat to their safety is external and, second, that their safety and security are also external. Turning the world and others into a projection screen of both danger and protection allows the Six to continue to give up their power because the sources of potential harm and potential shelter are both outside their control. The whole cycle of fear and mistrust can persist as long as the Six refuses to acknowledge that the call is coming from inside the house and that the source of their fear is internal.

The **Vice** of the Six is **fear,** which will compel them to either

cower and avoid perceived threats or run at them with the reckless-
ness and chaos of a drunken cast member on *Jersey Shore*. You'll
sometimes hear people talk about phobic Sixes and counterphobic
Sixes. Phobic Sixes (as the name might suggest) tend to expend
their energy by avoiding threats, whereas counterphobic Sixes tend
more toward a flat-out, *Braveheart*-style run directly at the source
of their fear in the hope of scaring it off by the sheer force of their
belligerence. There are a few working theories for why there are
two different types of Sixes.* But at the end of the day, what feels
most relevant for our purposes here is that, regardless of the approach, the underlying experience and motivation are the same:
fear and mistrust of self. And it's worth noting that all Sixes can
and do adopt both phobic and counterphobic tendencies, depending on the situation.

If you didn't skip ahead to read your own chapter, Type Six, you
may have noticed that in addition to explaining the Vice of each Type
as it relates to the rest of the ego structure, I like to stop and explain
the Vice's relationship to the dominant emotional experience of their
Center of Intelligence. If you skipped everything else and jumped
right to your chapter . . . now you know what you've been missing, I
guess? Anyway, I'm going to do that here. The Six manifestation of
this concept is a bit weird, so I guess the whole point of this paragraph is to issue a disclaimer. But Sixes love warnings and heads-ups,
so consider yourself forewarned. You're welcome.

So, if the Guardian's Vice (fear) is a response to their Head
Center's built-in dominant emotion (fear), that means that fear is
the Six's response to . . . fear. Ya see why I needed the long-winded
setup now? The pattern still tracks; it just needs a little extra explanation (but if I'm being honest, the Sixes were gonna want that
anyway). Fear, for all the Head Center Types, is oriented toward
the future: Will they be all right if they make a decision without all

---

*For the sake of transparency, I'll go ahead and say that I fall into the camp that sees
Instincts as an explanation for the *three* different versions of Type Six (not two).

the information, take a risk without having run a thorough-enough threat assessment of it, or commit themselves to a singular course of action and follow it through, forsaking all others, till death do them part? Informed by their ominous Core Belief, the Six is fixated on their safety and security: Will they survive this house of horrors we call the world? **Their ego structure's response to that fear is *more fear*, but it's less related to external threats and more preoccupied with their own perceived incapacity to face those external threats.** So, yes, there ya have it—the fear that is reflective of an absence of inner trust *is* the Six's response to their angst about their safety in this perilous world.

Sixes can be one of those Types that hold on to relationships for much longer than is healthy for them, out of fear of facing the unfamiliar, which awaits them on the other side. Sixes can also run out the clock on people's patience with their endless litany of questions and doubts, making their lack of trust in themselves everybody else's problem. And Sixes are afraid to take the next step forward, whether that next step is in the professional or personal arena. Instead, they stall out, mentally scanning for any possibility that they didn't already anticipate and furiously attempting to prepare for all the ways it could all go wrong.

One of the most frustrating patterns with Type Six is their constant questioning and interrogation of the other person, whether that person is a friend, a colleague, a child, a romantic partner, or the barista making their decaf iced latte (it is decaf, right?). Never satisfied with the first answer they get, the Six launches into their own personal Skeptic's Inquisition, endlessly querying and probing the people closest to them to reveal the covert motives that they have for wanting to be close to the Six. (Surely, they think, it can't be because there's anything endearing or charming about them; that can't be right.) Rejecting the notion that the people around them just like them and enjoy their company, the Six regards their friends, co-workers, and family members as very likely smooth criminals. They're slowly winning the Six over until their guard is down and they've finally begun to feel safe, and then they can blindside the Guardian.

It doesn't take a genius to see how this stubborn refusal to trust the people around them undermines the Loyal Skeptic's desire for closeness and devotion in their relationships. Predictably, the people closest to the Six grow weary from the constant interviewing of their character, every small inconsistency used against them in the dragged-out trial of their trustworthiness. By wearing people down and ultimately pushing them away with their accusations, the Six is often the principal architect in bringing into reality their worst fear of ending up alone and abandoned.

Strangely and somewhat paradoxically, another toxic pattern of the Six is their habit of remaining in relationships that aren't supportive and healthy for them, precisely *because* the devil you know is better than the devil you don't. There are a couple of key reasons that the Six will stay within harmful dynamics, rather than venturing out on their own. First, remaining in relationship with someone they can't trust because they've been untrustworthy confirms what the Guardian already believes about people: They're fickle and untrustworthy snakes who are looking out only for themselves! Having this solid evidence provides the Six with rationalization for continuing their cynical line of interrogation, their antagonistic doubting, and their relentless, cowardice-fed preparation in place of courageous action.

Second but no less critically, staying in inconsistent, subpar relationships (whether they're romantic, professional, familial, platonic, or with the barista who keeps making their iced latte with regular espresso instead of decaf) provides another function for the terror-stricken Six: the comfort of familiarity. Even if that familiarity is awful, it's predictable, and predictability isn't something that we humans get to enjoy all that often. Predictability provides some measure of security, because if the Six knows what is likely to happen next, they can at least prepare for it. So rather than venturing out on their own—and giving themselves the opportunity to grow trust in their capacity to survive without the routine of a predictably terrible relationship—they stay right where they are, taking yet another and another and another ride on the merry-go-round of hell.

While all Head Center Types share in the pattern of stalling out, delaying action in the form of the endless mental exercising (and exorcizing) of their anxiety, Sixes can be some of the worst offenders. They see every next step as a risk and run it through a risk appraisal, examining it over and over again for cracks in their mitigation plan. Even when they're given what by all accounts is a great opportunity, Sixes spiral into angst, afraid to take a chance on something new for fear of upsetting others, venturing into uncharted territory, or (if they make the horrible mistake of being successful) garnering negative attention and jealousy and ending up with a target on their back. Despite other people seeing their capacity to excel with more responsibility and leadership, Sixes shrink away from the opportunity to lead, not trusting themselves to meet the demands of the role and not trusting others to extend goodwill and loyalty to them if they hold authority or power. It makes sense that Sixes would shrink away from these roles, given that they naturally hold a lot of suspicion toward people in authority and power. But in backing away, they miss out on the opportunity to repair their relationship with power and contact their own inner badass authority that is naturally protective and preferential toward the underdog.

So how does a Six stop their relentless, frantic run on the hamster wheel of anxiety? How do they take a step forward without succumbing to the fear that they aren't prepared for whatever lies ahead? How do they

Your heroic rescuer isn't external. It's you.

relax into their relationships and trust that they're safe—without a Hunger Games–style trial of trustworthiness?

This is the part of the play where the Six's **Virtue** enters to rescue them from their self-imposed prison of endless preparation.

Please take note, sweet Six: Your heroic rescuer isn't external. It's *you*, baby; it's all you. The Virtue of the Six is **courage**: a grounded confidence in their ability to face whatever is up ahead, regardless of how much or how little they've prepared for it. Cultivating the Virtue of **courage means that the Six no longer gets stuck in their dress rehearsal for disaster but instead steps up and into action, steeled by trust in themselves.**

Courage demands that the Six stop looking outside themselves for safety, security, authority, and power. It redirects the Six to make contact with their own authority, agency, and wisdom in order to keep themselves and others safe. Courage rejects the notion that the Six is helpless in any way and instead gives them the kick in the can that they need to get out of their head and into the arena—taking risks without running endless calculations around the probability of disaster. Courage is Han Solo, in response to an anxious C-3PO reciting the probability of collision with an asteroid, saying, "Never tell me the odds," and steering the junk-bucket *Millennium Falcon* directly into the asteroid storm.

Now, Sixes, I know your instinct is to dismiss what comes next as cheap flattery, but I'm going to challenge you to have some faith that there are things about you that people love and appreciate. You show us what it is to be truly dedicated to something beyond ourselves, and you help us recognize that while certainty is an illusion, shelter and security can be experienced when we practice the courage to engage in the uncertainty. The gifts that you offer to the world are sound, solid guidance and the grounded, unconditional steadfastness of devotion as you navigate the people you love through the turbulence that comes standard-issue with the human condition.

I know that the chaos and uncertainty of your own life convince you that you'll be helpless without the protection of others, but it isn't all your endless preparation and risk-management drills that have gotten you to this point. No, my scrappy lil Sixes, it's your grit—the stubborn, willful force of your own determination to survive—that keeps you showing up and shepherding the people you love through the stormy waters of life to safer, more solid ground. When you stop looking everywhere outside yourself for your rescue, you're going to find that *you* are the one we all look to for guidance and safe passage.

All right, Sixes, you can finally relax. I'm done complimenting you. You survived without anyone else protecting you! See? I knew you could do it.

FROM BABY STEPS TO BADASS PATTERN BREAKING

Now, sweet Six, I'm going to encourage you to hold lightly the list of questions that follows. This isn't an exhaustive list, and I would contend that given your habit of interrogating everything you're told, you, more than any other Type, are uniquely qualified to come up with your own piercing, truth-revealing questions for yourself. So let this be just a jumping-off point; I can't wait to see how you hold your own feet to the fire like you do to the rest of us.

- Now, I know this is going to feel really counterintuitive to you, but I want you to suspend your disbelief in people's fondness for you for a moment. What do you think you're trying to protect by being skeptical of people's goodwill toward you? What would be at risk if you were to let down your guard and trust that people like you? And if people do actually like you, how do you think it affects them when you automatically disbelieve their fondness for you? What if people are loyal to you not just because you're ready for any disaster but because you're funny, warm, and spunky and give really good advice? What if I'm complimenting you right now not because I want something from you but because I want something for you— for you to trust in yourself as much as you try to earn the trust of others?
- So we just talked about your struggle to trust others, but we

know that at the heart of your reluctance to rely on others is an absence of trust in yourself. There's nothing inherently wrong with wanting to depend on the faithfulness of other people, but there's a fine line between wanting proof of people's trustworthiness and punishing them for what you can't seem to find within yourself. How is your constant suspicion of others turning your fear of abandonment into reality? What evidence for your own trustworthiness are you denying yourself by projecting your search onto everyone else? What do you need from yourself in order to trust yourself? And when you start to feel suspicion toward others stir within you, can you take that as an invitation to give yourself what you need in order to trust that you'll be okay, regardless of anyone else's choices?

BADASS PATTERN BREAKING

All right, my scrappy little Six, I know it feels safer for you to remain in the realm of risk mitigation, running drills in your head to prepare for every possible outcome (except the possibility of things going well), but that isn't what we're here for. You're so much more fierce and powerful than the small, helpless victim of circumstance that you resign yourself to being. These small shifts can help you start to see that. They're small risks that demand a vote of confidence in yourself, which will, with faithful practice, begin to add up in big ways. I believe in you. Now it's your turn to believe in yourself.

- At least once a week, commit to saying yes to someone else's suggestion, without asking any follow-up questions. I can feel you pulling back already, but hear me out: This isn't about the other person or their suggestion. It's about building confidence in yourself that you can walk into an unfamiliar situation, totally unprepared, and navigate it without disastrous consequences. This is about disrupting your pattern of thinking and overthinking and ultimately sitting out opportunities to show yourself what you're made of because it feels safer to imagine what could go wrong from the sidelines than to risk stepping out onto the pitch. Lace up your cleats, baby—Coach is putting you in.

- Learn how to trust compliments and accept them graciously, without suspicion. You're going to have to fake it till you make it on this one, but this kind of (unlicensed) exposure therapy will give you a sense of the things that people value about you that you're often too distracted by your fear to see in yourself. The next time someone extends a compliment to you, instead of swatting it away with a snarky joke, I want you to respond with "Thank you so much—it means a lot that you would say that!" You don't have to trust it yet . . . but over time, trust will come.

- The next time you have a decision to make and you find yourself getting anxious and seeking out feedback from other people, pause and commit to a course of action that you came up with. This challenge isn't about trusting yourself to make the right decision. This small shift is meant to help you see that even if you didn't pursue the right course of action, you'll be able to navigate your way through the situation.

TYPE SEVEN

*The Paradoxical Paralysis of Making
Too Many Awesome Plans*

When I get the chance to present on the Enneagram, I like to present the Types in the same order that I've covered in this book: starting with Type Eight and ending with Type Seven. I do that because it's a very traditional way to present the Enneagram, but I *also* do it because nothing is more entertaining to me than making the impatient Type Seven wait until the end of the presentation to be in the spotlight. And right now, I know the Sevens are getting their revenge by skipping everything else in this book and starting with their chapter.

Actually, if you Sevens knew what was good for you, your real revenge would be in skipping this book entirely, because I'm about to try to hurt your feelings. But I'm sure you'll find some way to rationalize all the very valid critiques I bring up. So, either way, this Teflon Type will still get away relatively unscathed, despite my best efforts.

Sevens are hard to miss with their enormous energy and contagious enthusiasm for life. Playful, engaging in their communication, and quick with a joke or wild story, Sevens are fairly difficult to mistake for any other Type. That said, they themselves are often the last to realize that they're Sevens, not wanting to commit to identifying with just one Type. Because settling for just one Type means missing out on all the fun parts of all the other Types, and that sounds like a real buzzkill.

As each Center of Intelligence has its black sheep of a Type, the Seven is the upbeat, cheerful outlier of the Head Center, a stark contrast to the withdrawn and intense Five and the mistrusting and agitated Six. Each of these intellectual Types has a pattern of giving away their authority, searching for an external source of reassurance in which they can trust, and the Seven has the most well-disguised strategy of this self-soothing routine. Appearing confident and enterprising, the Seven cleverly camouflages their bid for reassurance by cloaking it as fun possibilities and exciting plans. They sell their mental scheming as a good time rather than the mapping of escape routes and trapdoors to help them wriggle free of any disappointment or roadblocks they might encounter.

The archetypal name often given to Type Seven is the Adventurer or the Epicure, and it tells us that they want to squeeze every drop of juice out of the orange that is their life. Thrills and novelty excite the Adventurer, and the appeal of seeking out the best that life has to offer is in everything they get to sample along the way. If you've ever gone out to eat with a Seven, it's unlikely that they've ordered just one thing. They want to get a representative smattering of the menu, so several appetizers and sides and a doctored-up entrée later, the Seven will somehow still have room for dessert and four more hours of conversation. Despite all their capacity for fun and adventure, my favorite feature of the Seven is that when it comes to spiritual wisdom and depth, they're somewhat of the dark horse of the Enneagram. You'll find some of the most profound observations coming out of their mouth, sandwiched in between their outrageous stories and inappropriate but still hilarious jokes (shout-out break to my colleague K. Monet here for her inappropriate and hilarious jokes and her profound spiritual wisdom). I have yet to meet a Seven who hasn't punched way above their wacky weight class when it comes to spitting out unexpected and brilliant universal insights about our existence.

Sevens, this is where things are about to take a turn for the rude, so it's probably a good time to get those justification muscles warmed up (jk, I know those muscles are always primed for a flex). Far from being all fun and games, Sevens have a pretty gnarly underbelly to their sunny and silly initial impression. Frustratingly unreliable, dizzyingly unfocused, and famously bad at following through on the ideas that they've gotten everyone excited about, Sevens can be just as much of a nightmare as they are a good time. Refusing to accept responsibility for their frustrations, they excuse away all their flakiness and sidestep facing the real impact of their flightiness on other people. Particularly self-aware Sevens might name their shortcomings so that you can come to expect them, but don't hold your breath for an apology.

Sevens are the ultimate teases of the Enneagram, getting everyone all hot, bothered, and on board with the brilliant idea or plan they're hyping up. They build up buy-in and enthusiasm for the scheme that, by all indications, they're spearheading . . . until it's actually game time. *If* the Seven shows up at all, they commandeer the whole show with a PowerPoint presentation that they threw together this morning, all the old plans out the window and abandoned. It bears repeating: That's *if* the Seven shows up at all. So how did we get here?

The **Essential State** of the Seven is **a focused condition of constancy that still grants them the freedom to experience life fully** and makes way for the beautiful gift of the Adventurer. It's not their enthusiasm or even their creativity but their capacity to see the potential in everything and everyone, making them brilliant visionaries for a brighter future. As a future-focused Head Center Type, the Seven has a foresight that perceives the incredible promise that has yet to unfold from a situation or a person. It's no wonder, then, that mature, healthy Sevens make incredible mentors (quick shout-out break to Denise, one of my dear early mentors and a fabulous exemplar of this very Essence).

I once heard a friend (shout-out break to Vanessa here) describe Sevens as being able to see the world in HD. Colors, sounds, people, emotions—all amplified and expressed fully. Honestly, it sounds like a pretty intense acid trip to me, but then again, a lot of people report experiencing ego death during an acid trip, so maybe the Sevens are onto something here.

LSD trip or not, the ability to perceive the yet-to-be-revealed potential around every corner, and the optimism to bring it forth, is the kind of stubborn, bullheaded hope that we need in the sometimes-disappointing world we experience every day. Sevens are head-in-the-clouds dreamers, with just enough of a disconnect from reality to allow them to imagine with abandon and conceive something truly groundbreaking.

This Essence is really quite remarkable, and I think we've all probably seen glimmers of it in the Sevens we know. But that pesky Debbie Downer known as reality has a nasty tendency to come in and kill the vibe. The **Core Belief** that rains on the Sevens' parade of potential is that **the world is just one big disappointment after the next, with limitations and mediocrity dashing dreams and cutting off at the knees what could be possible.**

For a Type that has a unique and expectant Essence inherent to them, that is a *bleak* Core Belief to carry around. But it also explains a lot about the flightiness and flakiness that many of us experience with ego-activated Sevens. They're an active and assertive Type, with an abundance of energy and an approach to getting their needs met that pushes against the environment. If the environment they perceive is an ultimately disappointing, underwhelming one, then eager Sevens are going to do everything they can to thwart the inevitable letdown. They chase thrilling detours and plot twists to at least end up with a good story to tell at parties later.

Epicures are famously bad at staying the course and following through on the exciting ideas they come up with. Half-completed projects and abandoned business plans litter the path behind them while they chase the most recent shiny fantasy to capture their brief attention span. It's maddening to people who make the mistake of thinking they can rely on Sevens, but when we put it into the context of their Core Belief, we can see that all the Houdini-esque escapism is just their attempt to avoid heartbreak over wasted potential. Once again, like with the Core Belief of every other Type, we can find compelling evidence that the world *is* a disappointing place of squandered possibility.

Sevens perpetually chase after the next temporary source of satisfaction to avoid experiencing disappointment at their own inability to realize unlimited potential.

As they search for proof to corroborate the conviction they already hold as capital-T Truth, their **Focus of Attention** goes to **anything novel and unfamiliar that they can turn into a projection screen for their fantasies.** Sevens perpetually chase after the next temporary source of satisfaction to avoid experiencing disappointment at their own inability to realize unlimited potential. This may seem like a contradictory strategy— seeking out exciting opportunities as a way to prove themselves right that the world is generally dissatisfying and restrictive. But by always being on the lookout for the next sexy lil distraction, Sevens will be unable to experience anything to its fullest depth, therefore avoiding the disappointing limitations of their attention span and their lack of emotional stamina.

The **Core Fear** of the Seven presents itself in two layers. The first is an external fear about the world that sort of camouflages the second, a more chilling internal reflection of that Core Fear. At the surface, the Adventurer will express **an anxiety about the world, that it's a place that puts limitations on them,** stemming the flow of their potential to a tiny trickle. But if you press them a little and scratch below the surface of their initial admission, they might admit they're afraid that they are their own stumbling block and that **the limitations come not from the external world but from *within* them,** their hopes and dreams smashed cruelly against their own rocks. The limitations aren't obstacles laid out by the external universe but instead are the spasms and groin pulls of their own underdeveloped muscular system of execution and follow-through.

So how does the terrified lil Adventurer dodge the fear that they'll be faced with their incapacity to fully express and experience their potential? They get to work crafting an **Idealized Self-Image** that is like a greased-up pig at the state fair: impressive in its agility and speed and, even if you can catch up to it, slick enough to slip right through your fingers before you can hold them to a singular plan or train of thought. **Adventurous, free, and having "a kind of soft anti-authoritarian stance,"** as Bea Chestnut says.* The Seven's mask is quite charming, until you've made the mistake of believing a word they've said.

The Idealized Self-Image is subtly distinct from the Essence of the Seven, and learning to spot the difference is crucial to shifting from ego to essence. For all of us, potential is this auspicious promise that has yet to be realized in us. While expressing our potential does often require some discipline and focused work on our part (or at least getting out of our own way), there is also often an element of right timing required in reaching potential, a variable that is entirely outside our control. The free flow of potential requires that we trust and be patient with its development. Does "patient" and "willing to delay gratification" sound like the Sevens you know?

Yeah, I didn't think so. That's because we're more often acquainted with the Idealized Self-Image of the Epicure—bouncing from adventure to adventure while planning their next three adventures, entirely missing the opportunity to be present to the moment they're currently in. Living life on the run, always having several escape plans up your sleeve, takes effort—a lot of it. That's the thing about the Idealized Self-Image (of every Type). Sustaining it takes a lot more work than relaxing into our Essential State, but it also maintains the delusion that we have control over more than we actually do.

---

*Beatrice Chestnut, *The Complete Enneagram: 27 Paths to Greater Self-Knowledge* (Berkeley, CA: She Writes, 2013), 144.

I imagine I already lost the Sevens a few pages back because they got distracted thinking about the better Enneagram book they want to write. But for those of you who are reading this chapter because you're close to a Seven and you want to understand them better, I'm going to carry on with this point so that you can maybe pass it along to them for me. Deal? Deal.

The critical point regarding the Idealized Self-Image is that it didn't appear out of nowhere just for a good time and it's not just for show. The Idealized Self-Image has been adequate in helping Sevens survive the disappointment and mediocrity of the world. By being adventurous and free-spirited, they've been able to seize moments that others might miss out on. By being lighthearted and fun, Sevens have been invited to all the best parties and events, winning people over and feeding off the energy of others' enthusiasm and delight in them and their antics. In short, Sevens' playful and anything-is-possible mask has allowed them to find light in the darkness and make it from one painful moment to the next without losing their excitement and expectation for the next adventure. Their Idealized Self-Image might be one of the more challenging ones to leave behind on their self-compassion journey, but reflecting on it with fondness and gratitude for how it helped them until now will make it a little easier.

In order to keep the ego structure at its fighting weight, the double-trouble **Defense Mechanism** of **idealization** and **rationalization** keeps the Seven easily distracted and stubborn in their insistence that their pattern of abandoning their plans before being faced with their own limitations is perfectly justified, regardless of what it costs them or anyone else.

We've all seen the idealization of the Adventurer in full swing, because it's often what's fueling the pressure campaign they subject people to when they're trying to get everyone on board with their newest scheme. Because *this* scheme is *the greatest* scheme they've cooked up yet. Not unlike the Four, the Seven has this tendency to romanticize the shiny or sexy thing that's right in front of them, dumping everything else until some different shiny or sexy thing sashays into their field of vision. **Idealizing something novel allows them to fantasize about what is possible.** It conveniently redirects their attention away from the hard work that the last subject of their fantasy would have required in order to bring it into alignment with the dazzling heights of their fantasy.

Quickly swooping in to put the finishing touches on the series of unfortunate events that idealization starts, **rationalization provides excuse after excuse for why their flakiness was not just acceptable but *necessary*.** They had to abandon the plan they had agreed to because, *duh*, the thing they're currently idealizing is obviously better than the original plan. I believe that Sevens believe themselves when they say each new plan they come up with is better than the last; they're not being disingenuous with us. It's just that they'll do anything to avoid having to face a process that will reveal to them their limitations.

By giving them an exciting new thing to attach all their hopes to and a seemingly valid excuse to toss aside everything else in pursuit of that thing, the gruesome twosome of idealization and rationalization helps keep the Seven's ego running and reproducing their unreliability over and over again. In some ways, their relentless optimism is admirable, until we pause and remember that it's fueled by a fear and mistrust in themselves and their ability to survive disappointment. If their Core Fear is that the call is coming from inside the house, then their Defense Mechanism allows them to never be home when the phone rings.

The **Vice** of the Seven is this sort of bottomless pit within them, traditionally known as **gluttony. No matter how many exciting experiences and adventures they pack into**

If their Core Fear is that the call is coming from inside the house, then their Defense Mechanism allows them to never be home when the phone rings.

Gluttony causes the Seven to fuss and strain against the emptiness, resisting the very thing that might actually bring them some relief.

their day, their inner emptiness growls like an unfed stomach, unappeasable in its groans for indiscriminate more. Gluttony causes the Seven to fuss and strain against the emptiness, resisting the very thing that might actually bring them some relief, much like an exhausted baby that refuses to sleep.

Gluttony both fuels and vindicates the Adventurer's exhausting patterns. Rather than surrendering to the disappointment of reality, the Seven lets gluttony take the wheel, going from attraction to attraction, wanting to feel full and present but always fleeing from the sorrow of wasted promise.

In addition, feeding the vicious cycle of flakiness and inconstancy that makes the rest of us want to throttle the Seven, gluttony serves as their response to their future-fixated FOMO. They can't miss out on something great if their gluttony never allows them to take a freaking break. When the Seven fears missing out on all the promise that the world beckons with, gluttony says "Hold my beer" and abandons the present moment in search of an even better moment. . . . Lather, rinse, and repeat.

Sevens, I'd pause here and check in on you to see how you're doing, but we both know that you're doing just fine and this is all gliding off your back like water off a duck. Must be nice. But since we've gotten through the mechanical structure of your bullshit, let's take a few minutes to talk about what that looks like, on the ground, as it affects your relationships.

Flakiness and inconsistency are hallmarks of the Seven, but that wouldn't be possible without their pattern of foisting their wild fantasies on everyone else like they're some finance bro trying to sell you on cryptocurrency on a first date. Unfortunately for us, the Seven is way more convincing and charismatic than the finance bro. Their earnest enthusiasm is contagious, setting the trap for us to believe in them because they seem so wholeheartedly ardent about the prospective adventure they're regaling us with. Their imagination is so creative and nimble that when they paint the picture for us, we're on the ride with them, not just witnessing but experiencing it—and their excitement—along with them. Their boldness and forward momentum win us over, and suddenly, we're fully invested in the Seven's dream, all because of their eager and inspiring sales pitch.

Alas, the disappointment they're trying to avoid is then handed off to us when we show up ready to follow the Seven's lead on their newest project, only to find a breakup Post-it note in the place where they should be (if we're lucky enough to even receive a note—half the time, the conflict-avoidant Seven conveniently forgets to let you know they've moved on at all). And where is the Seven? Doing the same damn thing they did with you yesterday: earnestly and sincerely selling some poor unsuspecting sap on their latest fever dream!

This frustrating cycle—the Seven's persuasive marketing campaign to garner support for their latest passion project, followed up by no action on their part—can take place in all arenas of their life, whether they're wooing a potential romantic partner, pitching a professional opportunity, or selling their friends on going in on a time-share together. But just because they're no longer interested in seeing the idea through doesn't mean that it serves no

The Seven isn't actually trying to gather support for their prospective projects; they're unconsciously trying to gather scapegoats to blame in anticipation of their inevitable failure.

function. The Seven is silly, lighthearted, and playful, but they aren't stupid. This pattern of teasing others with exciting prospects only to ghost them at the last minute allows the Seven to fantasize to their heart's content, scheming and dreaming with reckless abandon. Then, feeling trapped by the expectations and hopes of others, they have someone other than themselves to blame for why the plan never materialized. The truth of the matter is that the Seven isn't actually trying to gather support for their prospective projects; they're unconsciously trying to gather scapegoats to blame in anticipation of their inevitable failure.

Another convenient escape route out of facing their limitations is the aforementioned soft anti-authoritarian stance. As a free-wheeling, adventurous Type, it stands to reason that the Seven would have no interest whatsoever in being obligated to someone above them, such as a supervisor, who the Seven should theoretically report to, or below them, such as a subordinate, who the Seven should theoretically supervise. Neither of these positions is exciting to the Seven, and in fact, both come with way too many responsibilities and expectations. However, unlike a less socially charming Type who might resist external expectations with open hostility and rebellion (cough, Eights, cough), the Seven takes a more subtle approach. They artificially level the playing field so that we're all peers here and no one is in charge. We're all equal participants in this situation, whatever this situation may be. Similar to their practice of getting everyone on board and then running off to chase a newer, shinier plan, charming everyone out of any kind of structure of accountability allows the Seven to evade the responsibility and expectations that come with whatever their assigned role is—lest their limitations rear their ugly head.

We've looked at two of the more insidious patterns of the Seven: first, hyping everyone up and getting buy-in for a plan they'll never see through, and second, disingenuously removing very real hierarchies. Because when things go sideways, they'll blame others, having made them just as culpable as themselves (and sometimes even more so, because others should really know better than to take the Seven at their word). Ever the Houdini when it comes to difficult and painful outcomes, the Epicure wriggles free by deflecting responsibility and moving right along. Your disappointed feelings are your problem, not theirs; they're too busy on the next thing.

These patterns are bad enough on their own, costing the Seven opportunities that they might otherwise have access to, if people could only trust them to follow through. But when they're combined with the Seven's assertive and sometimes aggressive push for the resources and energy they need to turn their ideas into reality, the people they've solicited support from feel taken for a ride and frustrated by the Adventurer's impulsiveness and seeming carelessness with their impact on others.

Known for dodging follow-through, the Seven simply stays in the safer realm of their engaging intellectual world rather than risking the effort of bringing their dreams to life. As they continue this vicious cycle, they also continue to deny themselves the opportunity to build the emotional muscles for navigating disappointment, and this deficit becomes yet another limitation that the Seven must escape—in addition to all the other limitations they're constantly dodging.

So how does this shifty, unreliable Type intervene in their self-defeating patterns and find a way to be present and satisfied by what is in front of them? Sevens, I know you didn't read any of the other chapters in this book before skipping to yours, so we can drop the pretense and get right to the point. Freedom from the prison of your patterns comes from the cultivation of your **Virtue,** which is known as **sobriety.**

Yeah, Sevens, sobriety is a bit of a bummer of a Virtue, especially when you consider some of the more badass ones, like courage or honesty or even right action. But, hey, let's try that honesty out here for a minute. We just got done talking about your famous lack of follow-through, so you gotta learn how to walk before you can run, you know?

So what is sobriety in the context of functioning as the Seven's Virtue? On multiple occasions, I've had to reassure different Sevens that sobriety doesn't necessarily mean abstaining from a lil nightcap (though it's kind of cute that such an imaginative and intellectually brilliant Type would take something so literally). Anyway, **sobriety here is a steadiness that requires clarity, discernment, and discipline,** in contrast to the Seven's reckless and insatiable appetite for stimulation when their Vice of gluttony is running the show.

Sobriety frees the Seven from their fear of their own limitations.

Sobriety asks for more from the Seven than they often expect of themselves, calling forth a more focused, reliable, and responsible Epicure that already exists. Sobriety holds the Seven to a standard that they didn't realize they were capable of meeting, and perhaps paradoxically, sobriety frees the Seven from their fear of their own limitations. It gives them new confidence in their ability to be receptive to the entirety of the present moment, without needing to self-medicate on exciting plans or distractions.

Listen, my little free spirits, you have such an incredible gift without needing to put forth any effort. That is, if you would just trust that it's enough to simply reflect the potential that exists in the world, without having to hatch a bunch of schemes to force it to manifest itself before its time. You've lived enough life to see that, despite the endless possibility and promise in each moment, person, and situation, our world is littered with wasted potential. Great and heroic dreams are gathering dust on the shelf, while mediocrity is given free rein. Yet your stubborn hopefulness burns brightly on, inspiring others. There is something so beautiful about your battle-tested capacity for finding promise in people. Your perspective and vision alone compel us to step up into a version of ourselves that we couldn't have imagined but you always knew was in there, just waiting to be seen. We need nothing more from you than to be recognized for what we're truly capable of; that spark that you see in us and fan into flame is enough to change the whole world.

All right, Sevens, I know you like being the center of attention, but we've got to wrap up somewhere, and this feels about as good a place as any. I promise, you already have everything you need to nurture the promise that you can see in the world. You just need to slow down and let it catch up to you.

FROM BABY STEPS TO BADASS PATTERN BREAKING

There's a bit of a common joke that's made at Type Seven's expense, and it essentially pokes fun at your seeming lack of ability to be alone with your thoughts. But as I've already gone on record to say, I think that Sevens have a sneaky side of spiritual depth to them, so you actually might surprise yourself (and the rest of us) if you let yourself stay with a thought long enough for it to leave your head and land in your heart. Live into your *real* potential by engaging with these questions faithfully and completely, and then keep showing up to a practice of self-reflection that will support you in bringing your dreams into reality.

- Let's start with the fear of your own limitations, which results in your famous reputation for inconsistency and unreliability. You spend a lot of time coming up with excuses for why you didn't follow through on something. How else can you imagine that energy being used? What are you afraid will be revealed about you if something you commit to fails? What do you think is the cost of your inconsistency? What might you be able to discover about yourself if you can stay the course through frustration and setback?
- As lighthearted and freewheeling as you come across, sweet Seven, you carry around some heavy disappointment, undigested as a result of your low threshold for pain and your impatience with grief's ungovernable timeline. You're very good at convincing yourself that your pain isn't worthy of your time and energy, but what do you think is the cost of leaving your sadness unattended to? What are you afraid will happen if you do let yourself feel the full weight of your disappointment? What do you think are the impacts on your relationships when you resist making time and space for sadness and letdown to be expressed and witnessed? What is the consequence to you of bearing the responsibility for

keeping the mood light and cheerful for everyone? How might
you create space and freedom within yourself if you could find
the courage to sit with your heartbreak for as long as it needed
you to?

BADASS PATTERN BREAKING

All right, my silly little Seven, you love options, so I'm going to
give you a few to take for a test-drive. Obviously, these aren't the
only small shifts you can make to break old habits, but I want you
to resist your usual instinct to brainstorm other (better, more exciting) ideas. Don't turn this into more of an intellectual exercise than
a real-life one. This is an invitation to cultivate your Virtue of sobriety. Stay with these, and give them a few honest tries, as they're
written, before you start scheming how to make them more interesting. It's my turn to surprise you with just how powerful a few
simple, small shifts can be.

- Pick a small, boring task every day, and commit to seeing it
  through. Make your bed every morning, clean the dishes every
  night, run the vacuum through the house, lay out your clothes
  for the next day—start something and finish it completely. You
  can pick something different every day, but be sure to do it to
  completion. Prove to yourself that you can be consistent and
  reliable, especially with something mundane.
- Limit yourself to one option. Start small. Commit to ordering
  only one meal the next time you go out for dinner, instead of
  building your own entrée sampler; keep only one flavor of ice
  cream in your freezer at a time; buy the sweater in only one
  color. Commit to something small, and give yourself the
  opportunity to come to appreciate it for its simplicity. Pay
  attention to what kind of clarity and insights become available
  to you when you limit yourself to one thing, rather than
  overstimulating yourself with all the options. Yes, even a

sweater in a single color can be a gateway to incredible spiritual clarity, if you give it a chance.

- Every Seven I've ever known has, while going through something devastating, insisted that they were okay. When you're going through something painful, I want you to let someone you trust see that you're not okay. Give yourself permission to be hurt, betrayed, angry, sad, and whatever else comes with the painful circumstances you're navigating. Let people show up for you, and let yourself be supported when you're not okay, instead of soldiering on alone, swallowing the pain whole. We know you'll be okay again, but you can give yourself permission to not be okay right now.

CONCLUSION

Ya made it through, ked. You survived. Hell—I survived! I can't believe I wrote an entire book. But here we both are, at the end of it. I wish I had something more profound to offer you to wrap this whole thing up, but I just wrote a whole book, so you're going to have to excuse me for limping over the finish line. But maybe it's a good thing for *my* power-hungry little ego, if I let this go out with more of a whimper instead of a bang, you know?

Speaking of my power-hungry little ego, I'm going to take a page out of the Six's book and project a fear of mine onto you, dear reader. Lest you've reached this point and come under the delusion that I'm some kind of enlightened Enneagram expert preaching at you from some higher consciousness, let me rid you of that nonsense right now. I'm right here in the trenches alongside you. We're in this together, babe, and I get it wrong—regularly. Just ask my colleagues. Or my friends. Or my family. Or my axe-throwing-league members. Or anyone I've dated in the last twenty years. They'll tell you that the only thing I'm an expert in is goofing up and missing the mark (in fairness, though, the axe-throwing-league members talk about me missing the mark on the target board *and* missing the mark on being a better, undefended version of myself, so just make sure you figure out which mark they're referring to when you ask them).

My point in that little overture is that, in all humility, I want you to know that I'm not some coach yelling plays at you from the sidelines. I'm your teammate, and I'm in the scrum with you, getting tackled and fouled and having my mouthguard knocked out right next to you. It's an honor for me to be trusted to offer my Enneagram insights while you're on your sacred self-compassion journey. And I'm incredibly proud of all of us for showing up every day in a world that keeps telling us why we shouldn't love ourselves.

We've covered a lot of ground on the bad behavior of all nine Types, and it can be brutal enough to face our shadow side alone, from the privacy of our midlife crises, never mind the humiliation of having it laid bare for anyone with a library card to read about. But the truth is that our shadow side has been out there for everyone in our lives to witness for a lot longer than this book has been in print. It's not some buried secret that only a few people have access to. The people in your life are just as capable of writing the chapter about your Type as I am—I just got to it first.

If that sounds even more mortifying, then let me offer you this reframe: The people in your life already know about and have been on the receiving end of your shadow side, yet *they're still here.* They still love you. They still know that there is more precious than patterned to you, and they're willing to take the good with the bad. My deepest hope for you is that you can radically accept yourself in the same way.

I know I've written it over and over again, but I think it's probably the most important thing in this whole book, so it bears repeating one last time for the road. None of our defensive postures and patterns came out of thin air. We live in a world that is lonely, disappointing, unsafe, and bleak, and we had to survive it somehow. We had good reason to become vigilant, self-sacrificing, evasive, and controlling. With the information we had at the time, we did the best we could, and it's no small miracle that we're still here today to tell the tale, no matter how cringeworthy that tale is to us now.

I hope I've lived up to my promise to be rude to you, and I hope I've made you laugh at yourself along the way. More than that, though, I hope that as you observe yourself and begin to see all the specific ways you're trying to navigate this big, bad world, you can have some compassion for yourself. You're doing the best that you can with what you have available to you. You've survived, and as long as you keep doing that, you'll have a chance to do better next time. You can do this—*we* can do this. I believe in us, and I'm so grateful to have you on this journey with me.

ACKNOWLEDGMENTS

So, *so* many people have supported me in bringing this book from a distant dream that I was terrified to admit to anyone, into the concrete binding of pages that you hold in your hands today. I'm sure that I'll wake up abruptly in a cold sweat, months after this manuscript has gone to production, realizing that I didn't include someone very dear to me in this section. I sincerely apologize and will make it up to you by naming my next pet after you. Deal? Now let me give this my best shot.

Considering that the Enneagram is a hot topic right now, I'm sure it's no surprise to anyone that there is a very robust field of Enneagram teachers, authors, and practitioners out there who are expanding how we think about and use the Enneagram every day. I feel very grateful to have access to both very traditional Enneagram teachings and innovative new perspectives that are broadening understanding and application of this amazing tool. This book wouldn't have been possible without the scholarship and contributions of several giants in the Enneagram world: David Daniels, for his work on the Basic Propositions; Russ Hudson and Don Riso, for their incredibly thorough Type descriptions and the Levels of Development; Helen Palmer, for her work on the Vice-Virtue Conversion; Richard Rohr, for his faithful and compassionate writing on the practical spirituality of the Enneagram; Sandra Maitri, for her work on the Passions and Virtues of the Enneagram; Chichi Agorom, for her brilliant and liberatory reclaiming of the Enneagram; and Sarajane Case, for her practical framework and application of the Enneagram in her writing, for her beautifully compassionate writings to each Type through her poetry, *and* for being an incredible example of graceful and gracious social media notoriety for me to look to and attempt to emulate. The writings of these teachers (and all the teachers and peers that I've learned the Enneagram from) are the foundations on which my work is built, and I'm grateful for the way they brought the Enneagram into the world with such depth and profound creativity.

From an incredibly practical perspective, this book couldn't have happened without my wonderful literary agent, Andrea Heinecke. Out of the blue, during a difficult moment in my Enneagram career, an email from Andrea arrived in my inbox with an opportunity to work with her and take the first steps on what has turned out to be an incredible journey. Andrea's patience with me while I began to craft a proposal; her wisdom, encouragement, and guidance as we went through the submission process; and her advocacy of me and my proposal as we received and negotiated the final offer were the foundations on which this book was built, and I'm eternally grateful to her.

Of course, this book couldn't have happened without a courageous editor and publishing house willing to take a risk on a first-time author and full-time internet smart-ass, and for that leap of faith, I'll never be able to thank Becky Nesbitt, Leita Williams, and the entire amazing team at Convergent enough. Before I had even signed a contract with Convergent, Becky's wisdom and encouragement gave me not only greater clarity on the particular tone I could take in this book but also the permission to take that tone without apology. Leita's sound guidance and counsel through the production and marketing process was a lighthouse piercing the darkness of a totally unfamiliar landscape for me, and I am so grateful for it! Immense thanks also to the many others at Convergent and Random House who touched this book, including Tina Constable, Campbell Wharton, Jessalyn Foggy, Alisse Goldsmith-Wissman, and Rachel Tockstein. The total support and enthusiasm from the Convergent team from the jump made me want to write a book worthy of their affirmation.

The list of colleagues and students at Wake Forest University (many of whom have become friends more than just co-workers or students) who have supported me, given me space to practice, and patiently listened to my endless Enneagram ramblings is long, and I'm certain I'll miss important people in my attempt to name names, but let's give it a shot, shall we? My immediate colleagues in the Chaplain's Office—Dr. Tim Auman, Dr. Gail Bretan, Naijla Faizi, Dr. K. Monet Rice, Pattie(cakes) McGill, Christine Yucha—you've all been witness to this wild ride and supported me in finding ways to lean into this new landscape. For all the ways you've supported my journey, I would need to dedicate an entire chapter to you, so I hope it will be enough for me to say how immensely grateful I am for each of you. Shelley Sizemore, Dr. Marianne Magjuka, Heidi Robinson, Dr. Chris Copeland, John Champlin, Dr. Cherise James, Justin Sizemore, Davita DesRoches, Cameron Steitz, Allison Thompson, Maij Mai, Gabriel Samuel, Alison Hoffer, Alex Morgan, Morgan Briggs, Dr. Francis Sto. Domingo, Hannah Montague, David Hooker, Janay Williams, Marilla Morrison, Grace Russell, Joe Sposato, Isabella Ryan, James Franklin, Dr. Chris Towles, Andrew Boyd, Chris Horne, Brandon Lokey (and, of course, David), Brian Calhoun, Shula Cooper, Fr. Marcel Amadi, Gregg Cecconi: Your encouragement and celebration of me at every stage of this process have been a lifeline and a reminder to enjoy the ride, and I can't thank you enough.

Over the course of my life, I've been fortunate enough to cross paths with some of the best human beings, who have shaped me into the person I am today. Brendan Rauth, there is nothing I could say that will adequately express the love I have for you and the appreciation I have for our friendship—this space that we have cultivated over the years has given me the safety and security to be vulnerable and to allow myself to be seen fully. I'm proud of the friendship we've created and the people we've become because of it.

Virginia and K. Monet, I dedicated this book to y'all, so you already know I have an abundance of gratitude for you, but let me expand on that real quick: From the very beginning of Rude Ass Enneagram, you both had this sturdy, grounded confidence in it and in me, that this would become something so much more than some snarky little Finstagram. The solid ground of your faith in me supported me through moments of my own doubt. Virginia, your honking laugh at my shenanigans always felt like a particularly satisfying endorsement of my weird sense of humor, and, K. Monet, I always knew I got it right when you told me to mind my business. You're both such badasses, and I'm so aggressively grateful to you.

Adwoa Asante, without our friendship and your brilliant observation about EnneaThought for the Day, there would be no Rude Ass Enneagram! Your thoughtfulness, intentionality, and humor are forces for good in this messy world, and watching you come into your own and radiate light and strength is nothing short of beautiful. You're a rock star, and I'm so grateful to call you my friend.

A number of my personal hometown heroes have been in my life since very early on, and their friendship and guidance have been invaluable across all the versions of myself that they have come to know: Lydia Sapp, Allison Keller, Olivia Sederlund, Lauren Sleeper, and Steve Lane, I'm so grateful for the longevity of my friendship with each of you. It's been so exciting to share this new chapter with friends who have known me since my awkward teenage days (and awkward first-grader days, in the case of Liv!).

Vanessa Rivera, my Instagram friend turned real-life friend, holy *moly*, have you been an integral part of this whole wild ride. From early on, you clocked my softer side, knowing that it was just as present in my posts as my snark, and you cultivated a friendship that was safe enough for that part of me to be seen. When I encountered setbacks and disappointment in the Enneagram world, your perspective and wisdom helped anchor me safely through that turbulence. Thank you!

To the friends I've made during my time in North Carolina, especially Delton and Kelly Russell, Tyler and Anna Leaphart, Paul Collins, Matt Harris, Keri McGee, and, of course, my entire axe-throwing fam, I can't tell you how much it means to me to have you in my corner, celebrating each step of this wild journey with me. I'm so grateful for each of you!

To my personal trainer, Chris Chafin—it may seem strange for your name to show up in the acknowledgments of an Enneagram book, but it was through your consistent, positive, and supportive presence that this intense and battle-ready Type Eight came to learn that sustainable strength can be cultivated through affirmation and encouragement, perhaps even more than through adversity and struggle. For listening to me rattle on and on about the Enneagram Friday after Friday and for creating a strength-training environment in which it's safe for me to acknowledge my limits, I'm so very grateful for you.

Rachel, Devon, Melissa, and Molly—women who have trusted me with their struggles as we explored them through the lens of the Enneagram and taught me how transformational the Enneagram can be—your courage, humor, and willingness to face discomfort for the sake of growth have been an honor for me to witness. Thank you for your trust and for what you've taught me about the Enneagram!

A girl is only as good as her therapist and her spiritual director, and luckily, I have two of the best in their respective businesses. Katherine, when we started working together ten years ago, I couldn't have imagined the life I live today, and I'm so grateful for how you've supported me believing in myself enough to build the life that I still can't quite believe I have. Elle, the sensitivity, tenderness, and care that you accompany me with are healing and inspiring, and the way that you've encouraged me to dream beyond the safety of not getting my hopes up has made me more courageous with my optimism and confidence. I'm deeply grateful to you both!

Stonehill College was home to me from the moment I stepped on campus for my first tour, and the people I met there have had an enormous impact on who I am today. Denise Gannon, Tim Gannon, Maura Proulx Carpinello, MaryAnne Davey, LucyRose Moller, Sarah Linnell, Kathi Hannon (and, of course, Schwally, even though you're only honorary Stonehill)—you're just a few out of many who made an indelible mark on my life. Undeniably, I am who I am because of each of you, and I'm so grateful for your mentorship and friendship and what you each helped cultivate within me.

It may seem strange to include a handful of Winston-Salem small businesses in my acknowledgments, but I believe in the core of my being that the Nashville hot biscuit at Krankies, the emo music first thing in the morning at Anchor Coffee, the bologna breakfast sandwich and crispy potatoes at Acadia, the coffee and the cocktails at Footnote, and the iced Smokey the Bear at Chad's Chai (along with the generous care, hospitality, and delightful senses of humor found in Chase, Aidan, Micah, and the entire staff there) were critical factors in my writing process. Truly, Winston-Salem has so many amazing small businesses and amazing people working in them; I'm so grateful to live in a city with so many places for me to post up and write this book into existence.

Second to last but certainly not least, a note of the deepest, most sincere gratitude to my family—Mom, Dad, Alexandra, and, of course, Admiral, Zeus, Finn, and my sassy lil Ollybear. You've been present and cheering me on at every turn that my life has taken (maybe not you, Zeus, but I won't take it personally). Thank you for . . . Well, I'd need to write another book to sufficiently take inventory, so for the sake of brevity—thank you for everything, truly. None of this would have been possible without you.

And finally, I can't end this book without expressing not just gratitude but deep affection for everyone who has followed @RudeAssEnneagram over the years. When I began, I could have never imagined it would lead me down this path, but without you and your support, I would be just another ding-dong with an Instagram account. For sharing your struggles with me during Tough Love Tuesdays, for sharing my posts with your friends and family, and for giving me the opportunity to bring a sense of humor into the profound work of the Enneagram, thank you. This book is my love letter to you—thank you *forever* for your support.

ELIZABETH ORR originally hails from the famous but sleepy New England town of Concord, Massachusetts, where she grew up as a strange mix of theater kid, track-and-field jock, and orchestra nerd (or dorkestra nerd, as she lovingly refers to it). After completing her bachelor's and master's degrees in her home state, Orr moved down to Winston-Salem, North Carolina, in 2014, where she has served in the Chaplain's Office at Wake Forest University. She started @RudeAssEnneagram in 2018 as a silly little outlet for her love of the Enneagram and for her standard issue Type Eight full-contact sport sense of humor. As the account grew, Orr pursued formal training as a practitioner of the Enneagram so that she could continue to roast people with more and more devastating accuracy. When she's not making people regret that they followed her Instagram account, Orr loves cooking, strength training, competitive axe-throwing, water aerobics classes, hunting for vintage Pyrex, brewery musical bingo and trivia, and taking long, meandering walks downtown with her sassy little pup, Olive.

ABOUT THE TYPE

This book was set in Caslon, a typeface first designed in 1722 by William Caslon (1692–1766). Its widespread use by most English printers in the early eighteenth century soon supplanted the Dutch typefaces that had formerly prevailed. The roman is considered a "workhorse" typeface due to its pleasant, open appearance, while the italic is exceedingly decorative.